"What if your city were converted in[...] overnight? How would you r[...] envy, online dating, and wai[...] ok can make your city shine, an[...] wish you did. It's about mindf[...] [...]ep, curious, and full of fun."

> —Christopher K. Germer, Ph.D., clinical instructor at
> Harvard Medical School and author of *The Mindful
> Path to Self-Compassion*

"Jonathan Kaplan's *Urban Mindfulness* is an engaging, useful, and enlightening guide to living in a world that often seems filled with pressure, chaos, and tension. This is a book that you can use every day to help you find peace and purpose in the smallest but most important moments of your life. There is peace out there, and it comes from within."

> —Robert L. Leahy, Ph.D., director of the American
> Institute for Cognitive Therapy and clinical professor
> of psychology at Weill Cornell Medical College

"Although city living can be stressful, it also provides us with many opportunities for reflection and insight. This book reminds us that we can discover tranquility within ourselves and connection in the city itself. It is an excellent guide with many helpful suggestions on how to do just that."

> —Sharon Salzberg, author of *Lovingkindness*

"In *Urban Mindfulness*, Kaplan provides a host of ways to practice being aware, without judgment, in the present moment, in the midst of busy, complex, city-based lives. This book can serve as a useful, practical resource for anyone interested in cultivating mindfulness within the context of their lives, as opposed to during a remote retreat. The wide range of exercises, such as the subway meditation and mindful texting exercise, ensures that readers will find several practices that speak to them."

—Lizabeth Roemer, Ph.D., professor of psychology at the University of Massachusetts Boston and coauthor of *The Mindful Way Through Anxiety*

"Many thanks to Kaplan for offering so many practical and rewarding ways to be more mindful in urban environments. In this easy-to-use book, he reminds us that being mindful is simply about being aware and present and it is not dependent on, or limited by, where we are or what we are doing."

—Jeffrey Brantley, MD, author of *Five Good Minutes* and *Calming Your Anxious Mind*

URBAN mindfulness

cultivating
peace, presence
& purpose
in the middle
of it all

Jonathan S. Kaplan, Ph.D.

New Harbinger Publications, Inc.

Publisher's Note

Distributed in Canada by Raincoast Books

Copyright © 2010 by Jonathan Kaplan
New Harbinger Publications, Inc.
5674 Shattuck Avenue
Oakland, CA 94609
www.newharbinger.com

Cover design by Sara Christian; Text design by Michele Waters-Kermes; Acquired by Melissa Kirk; Edited by Nelda Street

Library of Congress Cataloging-in-Publication Data

Kaplan, Jonathan S.
  Urban mindfulness : cultivating peace, presence, and purpose in the middle of it all / Jonathan S. Kaplan.
       p. cm.
  Includes bibliographical references.
  ISBN 978-1-57224-749-9
  1. Stress (Psychology) 2. Stress management. 3. Meditation. 4. City and town life. I. Title.
  BF575.S75K367 2010
  158.1'2--dc22
                                    2010020703

FSC

Mixed Sources
Product group from well-managed
forests, controlled sources and
recycled wood or fiber

Cert no. SW-COC-000952
www.fsc.org
© 1996 Forest Stewardship Council

All Rights Reserved. Printed in Canada.

12   11   10

10   9   8   7   6   5   4   3   2   1   First printing

This book is printed with soy ink.

With love to Eli and Baby Reed, who inspire my practice and let me know—quite vocally—whenever my attention has wandered from the present moment.

Contents

Out and About 113

Anytime, Anywhere 145

References 177

Acknowledgments

I would like to express my deep gratitude to the many people who encouraged, supported, and guided me as I wrote this book. From the outset, my editors at New Harbinger, Melissa Kirk and Jess Beebe, impressed me with their constructive suggestions and helpful feedback. Their collective expertise in content and style have made this a better book than it would have been otherwise.

The writings and practices of many profound teachers, including the following, have influenced my own personal journey in contemplative practice: Henry David Thoreau, D. T. Suzuki, Morihei Ueshiba, Sharon Salzberg, Thich Nhat Hanh, H. H. the Dalai Lama, and Pema Chödrön. In addition, the courage and dedication of the pioneers who introduced Buddhist practices and Asian healing approaches to American psychology continue to impress me, including Herbert Benson, Jon Kabat-Zinn, Jack Kornfield, Ellen Langer, Marsha Linehan, Alan Marlatt, and David Reynolds, among others. I also appreciate the wonderful example my friend and mentor, Bob Leahy, sets by doggedly pursuing what matters, even when confronted by setbacks.

I am indebted to my clients, who have given me the privilege of helping them through very difficult times. Seeing their perseverance and hard work in therapy inspires me to do my best and be the best psychologist I can be. It has been an honor to serve them.

I am also fortunate to have enjoyed the support of so many friends and colleagues that it's impossible to mention them all here. I would be remiss, however, if I didn't thank the following people: Joe DeCola, for sharing the joys and travails of being a dad; Sunna Jung, for sharing an appreciation of what's for lunch; Fred Weiner, for sharing life in the country; Lee Coleman, for sharing a passion for zombies; Mark Becker and Andrés Montoya, for sharing a beer; and whichever Facebook friend turned me on to the cat (as in feline) that plays keyboards.

I would also like to express my gratitude to Lybi Ma and the other editors at the *Psychology Today* website for their support of the Urban Mindfulness blog.

I want to especially thank Jennifer Egert, Rob Handelman, and Irene Javors, who have tirelessly and patiently contributed to urbanmindfulness.org. Together, with the insightful comments of our dedicated blog readers, we have shown the importance of bringing mindfulness to city living and have created our own online community.

My parents, sister, and in-laws were wonderfully supportive of me during the writing process. Whether by coming all the way to New York to lend a hand or by sending care packages (including the comics), they were there for me every step of the way. I feel tremendously grateful for their love. And, though it pains me to say this, the periodic reminders to "Get a haircut!" were helpful too.

Words cannot express my gratitude and love for my wife, Doris. She has provided unconditional support, tireless editing, and selfless accommodations for my work. Her love has sustained me in times of doubt, and the freshly baked bread hasn't hurt either.

Finally, I want thank my fellow New Yorkers. Though it's hard to appreciate when we're jammed into a crowded subway car, we share the same path in seeking happiness and well-being. By acknowledging our inherent similarities and honoring our differences, we can unite in cultivating a more mindful, compassionate society.

Introduction

Several years ago, I moved to New York City from rural Ohio. Before living in Ohio, I lived in big cities all over the world, including Boston, Tokyo, San Francisco, and Los Angeles. But my time in Ohio was my first experience of small-town life. Working as a professor and psychologist in a college town, I enjoyed both my five-minute commute to work and all the free time I could devote to family, friends, exercise, gardening, meditation, and mindfulness practice. My life was remarkably stress free and—dare I say?—balanced. However, I missed the excitement, culture, and variety of the city. When I wanted to savor some fresh sushi or see the latest traveling art exhibit, there was no place to go. Lured by these opportunities and a new job, I left country life and headed back to the city.

When I came to New York, I reveled in my new life and experiences. There was so much to do and see, and I was excited about this urban adventure. As a psychologist, I saw dozens of clients every week and found most people very receptive to learning about mindfulness. But my own sense of peace and balance gradually began to unravel, and I started feeling stressed and tired. I dreaded my long, crowded subway commute, and the cacophony of honking horns, car alarms, and ambulance sirens bothered me. I started to feel pressed to do things faster, yet complained of having too little time. One day, I noticed myself walking and talking just as quickly as the "uptight" New Yorkers around me, and griping when people didn't move out of my way or "get to the point." I watched my health start to decline as I exercised less and ate whatever I could grab on the go. Even my commitment to meditation waned: I could not find the right space emotionally, mentally, and even physically in my small studio apartment.

Not surprisingly, I observed many of my clients struggling with the same issues. They wanted to reduce stress and feel a sense of calm in the city, but there was just too much to manage. Starting and maintaining a meditation practice was very difficult. Vacations, yoga, and spa visits helped, but their therapeutic effects were short lived. Retreats for meditation and community provided a welcome respite, but eventually my clients had to face returning to "real life" in the city.

Besides complaining about daily hassles, my clients spoke of more significant difficulties. They talked about feeling lonely and isolated, despite being surrounded by people day and night. They described feeling burned out from the competitiveness they perceived at work, while dating, or even standing in line at the movies. Some spoke of the financial strain of living in one of the most expensive cities in the world and how they had to work so hard to stay afloat. Despite earning a decent salary, they saw their paychecks seemingly evaporate after covering household expenses. Even people who had significant financial resources weren't immune to city stress. They resented having to be available by phone, e-mail, and text message 24/7, while feeling unable to enjoy their earnings. After dealing with these stresses over time, many started to feel anxious, depressed, irritable, and completely overwhelmed, which was often when they arrived at my office door.

As any well-trained psychologist would do, I resumed reading books and studies on stress management, especially those focused on mindfulness. If you're unfamiliar with mindfulness, you can consider it to be a special way of paying attention. Disengaging from "automatic pilot," we consciously turn our focus to what's happening right now, in the present. For example, in this immediate moment, you're breathing while holding this book and reading this sentence, even though you may have groceries to buy, bills to pay, calls to make, and so on. Though mindfulness is often equated with meditation or a focus on breathing, it involves more than these practices. It helps you cultivate the ability to experience life as it unfolds through the practice of noticing your thoughts, feelings, sensations, and perceptions unencumbered by thinking, evaluating, rejecting, or clinging. Mindfulness also engenders a gentle curiosity about such experiences, which necessarily requires openness and acceptance. Instead of getting wrapped up in what "should" or "shouldn't" be, for example, mindfulness encourages us to become aware of the way things *are*, including the degree to which we might be judging—or even ignoring—our experiences. Put simply, mindfulness is:

- Noticing your thoughts, feelings, and actions without judgment or criticism

- Observing what's happening around you

- Being fully aware of your senses moment to moment

- Living in the here and now without resorting to old patterns and automatic reactions

- Exercising acceptance of your own experience, whether good, bad, or neutral

Mindfulness is often misidentified as exclusively a Buddhist concept, but more correctly, it's part of all spiritual traditions. Within Christianity, for example, the centering prayer aims to cultivate an inner stillness, better enabling communion with God. In Judaism, Shabbat, the holiest day of the week, sanctifies the practice of merely being rather than working or creating anything. Further, psychology has adopted mindfulness in a secular fashion over the past few decades. Various scientific studies have identified the benefits of mindfulness and meditation in treating chronic pain, alcohol abuse, anxiety, and relapse in chronic depression (Kabat-Zinn 1990; Marlatt and Gordon 1985; Orsillo and Roemer 2005; Segal, Williams, and Teasdale 2002).

Given these benefits and the fact that not only my clients but I, too, suffered from the stresses of city living, it made sense for me to rededicate myself to mindfulness practice. I pored over scientific articles and books by many experts on mindfulness. In Buddhist texts, I found tales of sitting in the forest, riding horses, and practicing falconry, which weren't particularly relevant to urban experiences of eating on the go or driving in traffic. Many mindfulness-based therapies also seemed impractical. They empha-sized spending up to an hour daily in meditation, which, although an incredibly helpful practice, proved to be too much of a hurdle to those of us struggling with limited time and energy. So, while there were some helpful insights, I found that none of the resources quite adequately addressed the unique experiences, opportunities, and challenges of urban life. This discrepancy isn't that surprising, given that many of the authors (monks, mindfulness experts, and the like) lived in rural or monastic communities, removed from the busyness and chaos of modern city life. So where does this leave the rest of us? How can we nurture our own practice of mindful-ness while continuing to live and work in the city? Are there ways for us to become aware and present without—or despite—feeling overwhelmed? Can we find ways to practice mindfulness other than sitting on a meditation cushion or a therapist's couch?

Asking questions like these, I realized we needed to find better ways to practice mindfulness in the city. Drawing on its princi-pal foundations, I knew we could develop ways to become more mindful—and even to meditate—in the context of our everyday experiences. Instead of just talking about "loving thy neighbor" in church or practicing loving-kindness in the *sangha* (meditation community), we could be compassionate toward our fellow subway riders and the homeless people we see each day. We could meditate while strolling through the park, running to catch the bus, or even petting a dog. It was from this perspective, as well as my desire to help clients, friends, and myself, that *Urban Mindfulness* was born.

Initially, I started writing a blog about ways to be more mindful in the city (urbanmindfulness.org). Readers started visiting the website with insightful, encouraging comments, and I realized there was an audience interested in applying mindfulness practice to urban living. Soon afterward, a few like-minded professionals began contributing pieces as well. Our readership continued to grow, and I was invited to start blogging for *Psychology Today* (www.psychologytoday.com) on the same topic. The number of visitors and readers continued to climb, and I realized urban mindfulness was more than just a concept, a blog, or a website. We had become a community dedicated to mindfully experiencing our lives. Join us, won't you?

In this book, you'll find tips, reflections, and guidelines designed to support your mindfulness practice in the city. The following fifty chapters provide practical suggestions reflective of our shared experience of urban living. They come from my own personal experiences, professional work with therapy clients, and insights drawn from being part of the urban mindfulness community. I encourage you to try various exercises to see what works best for you, given your own lifestyle and circumstances.

To facilitate your practice, this book is divided into parts that relate to *where* you might practice mindfulness: "At Home," "At Play," "At Work," "Out and About," and "Anytime, Anywhere." "At Home" draws from common experiences that we have in our living spaces. For example it tackles the dilemmas of having too little space, too little privacy, and too much clutter. "At Play" advises how to bring mindful attention to our recreational experiences, whether visiting a museum or exercising. By reconnecting with the inherent enjoyment associated with play, we can have more fun and relieve stress more effectively. "At Work" addresses the common kinds of experiences and settings we're likely to have on the job, whether we work in an office, restaurant, or retail store, or even outdoors. In most of these settings, we want to have friendly relationships with coworkers and practice mindfulness in ways that don't interfere with what we're hired to do. "Out and About" provides guidelines for practice as we move around the city—for example, meditating on the subway or mindfully walking down a busy, crowded street. We can approach many common urban experiences, like encountering homeless people or street musicians, in ways that embody our dedication to mindfulness. And finally, "Anytime, Anywhere" includes exercises to do and reflections to consider regardless of where we are and what we might be doing in the city. Because they don't require us to be in any particular place, these exercises invite you to practice mindfulness in ways consistent with almost any situation, such as when you text a friend or hear a siren. The fifty chapters aren't meant to be read sequentially but, rather, to be considered individually so you can focus on whichever parts seem most relevant to you at a particular time. So if you don't have small children, you might skip the chapter "Toddler Time" and go to "Mindful Messaging" to learn how to mindfully send text messages. Later in your life, if and when you have children, you might decide to revisit this book and read that chapter you missed.

I wish I could say that these exercises fixed everything for my clients, readers of the Urban Mindfulness blog, and me, that we never feel stressed, lonely, or overwhelmed, but that's not the case. There continue to be days in which my blog readers want more green space. My clients still talk of feeling lonely sometimes. And every so often, I find myself longing for a little peace and quiet. However, we've found some relief by becoming more mindful, accepting, compassionate, and grateful while remaining grounded during our experiences. Reacting with more equanimity and realizing important personal goals in the now provide a new perspective and help us have more mindful moments. In particular, the realization has come about that every day in the city is a new opportunity for practice as we travel down the same noisy, busy, crowded streets together. Through this book's advice and support, combined with your intention and commitment to practice mindfulness, you'll be well on your way to cultivating peace, presence, and purpose while living in the middle of it all.

At Home

Meditation at Home: A Dialogue Between Inner and Outer Spaces

Scene: In a city apartment, someone prepares to meditate. Sunlight spills through the window as the day dawns: 7:32 a.m.

Inside.   *Time for practice. Just need to take my seat and settle down now. Oops, two minutes late!*

Outside.   [Crack!]

Inside.   *Ouch! What was that? My knee? Oh, no, not again! I hope it's not—oh, whew! It doesn't really hurt. Okay, so where was I? Ah, yes, sitting. Sit up straight, review my intention—I intend to rest my attention on my breathing—and breathe. When thoughts arise, I'll let them go and return to my breath.*

OUTSIDE.   [Woo-woo-woo!]

INSIDE.   *A fire engine? Wow, that's really loud! It'll be gone in a minute. I'll just wait. Going, going, gone. Now, back to the breath.*

OUTSIDE.   [Rumble; ee-ur, ee-ur, ee-ur, woop-woop-woop!]

INSIDE.   *Stupid car alarm! That thing always goes off whenever I try to concentrate. I wish it'd just get stolen, already.*

OUTSIDE.   Hey, whatcha doing?

INSIDE.   *Oh, look who wandered in! What does it look like I'm doing? Huh? Maybe if I breathe really loudly, you'll get the hint.*

OUTSIDE.   Oh, meditating, huh? Okay, let me just get something for a second [bang].

INSIDE.   *Go away, already. I can't concentrate. This has got to be the worst meditation ever. Wait a sec— didn't I say that last time?*

Recognizing the physical, emotional, mental, and spiritual importance of meditation, many of us try to meditate at home. However, when you live in the city, creating the ideal atmosphere at home can be frustrating, if not impossible. We have to deal with excessive noise, little space, and the potential for unending distractions. It's bad enough when we have only our thoughts to distract us, but worse when the outside world also seems to conspire to undermine our practice. Regardless of the source, it's important to recognize that getting distracted is normal. In fact, it's the raw material of meditation: we focus our awareness on some aspect of the present moment and return our attention to it whenever the mind wanders. It's a relatively simple process, but not easy. If it were, there'd be no need to meditate!

To address these challenges, here are a few tips to help you structure your home meditation experience a little better:

- Create a pleasant, uncluttered space. Depending on the size of your home, maybe you're limited to claiming a small corner of the bedroom or, if you're lucky, you have a whole room to yourself. Either way, size doesn't matter. It's mainly important that your space be relatively clean and tidy. You don't want to meditate while staring at a pile of dirty laundry. You also don't need to be too concerned with decorating your space. Flowers, candles, or images can be inviting and supportive, but they're not required. In formal *zazen* meditation, people meditate while staring at a blank wall—not too inspiring, but it works.

- Establish a consistent time, ritual, or both for your home meditation. To best support your practice, it helps to meditate routinely at a particular time of day. Most people choose the morning, because it's generally quieter and our minds haven't quite gotten going yet. However, you can choose to meditate whenever is most convenient for you. Additionally, establish a small ritual to help you transition into the meditative state. Perhaps ring a bell, recite your reasons for meditating, or brew a cup of tea that steeps while you sit.

- Keep your meditation cushion, mat, or other supplies clean and protected. You don't want to leave your meditation cushion on the sofa, where something might get spilled on it. Try putting your meditation supplies in a special corner or in the closet. Keeping them covered and protected from dirt and dust also helps.

- Minimize external distractions. You can't control some things, like oversensitive car alarms, but you *can* limit some distractions and lessen the impact of others. For example, if your pet is too curious about your meditation, offer a few treats in another room just before you begin. If other people in your house are disruptive, talk to them beforehand, or arrange to meditate while they're gone. Also consider wearing earplugs or earphones if the noise around you is too distracting.

- Roll with disruptions. In any meditation session, you're bound to get distracted by stuff around you, bodily sensations, or thoughts going through your mind. So when you find that your mind has wandered, just return your attention to the subject of the meditation. Notice what's happening and your reaction to it. Accept that it's your reality right now, and keep returning your awareness to the meditation.

Mini Mindfulness
Masters at Home

Often, our search for inner peace and tranquility involves leaving home. We seek support from others by attending talks, meditating in groups, or retreating to the country. Alternatively, we might visit a website or bookstore in search of guidance in blogs, books, or magazines. However, we need not always pursue (and pay for) mindfulness experts in these settings. Sometimes, we can find the best mindfulness teachers in our own homes, literally underfoot. Pets and children have an uncanny ability to live fully in the present moment, thus they can serve as "mini mindfulness masters" to guide our practice. Cats, dogs, and babies each contribute their own unique teachings.

When you see a cat basking in the sunshine, it's easy to appreciate such mindfulness-related qualities as acceptance and sensual fulfillment. Reveling in the present moment, cats find contentment in the experience of napping in a warm, dry place. Rather than insistently dragging a well-loved toy nearby or striving for the perfect angle at which to sleep, the cat simply settles into the space. And when the sun passes, cats almost always continue napping in the shade, rather than chase the sun to another well-lit spot. Cats stretch to relish the warmth of the sunny day as it unfolds, without worrying about the chance of rain, or regretting bygone sunbeams.

Dogs are also wonderful teachers of mindfulness practice. They can demonstrate an enviable level of concentration and focus on the present moment. Don't believe me? Have you ever tried to eat lunch in front of a hungry dog? Salivating unabashedly, dogs focus visually on every bite of food as it travels from plate to mouth. Paying such exquisite attention to the process of eating is an integral part of several mindfulness-based psychotherapies (for example, Kristeller and Hallett 1999). Dogs' loyalty is a wonderful example of a relationship without criticism or condemnation. It doesn't matter what kind of day you've had, what you look like, or how your breath smells; you can be confident that your dog loves you unconditionally. Dogs don't pass judgment on you or set limits on when and how they express their affection for you.

With reactions unmitigated by expectations, babies, too, fully engage with the present moment. Given their nascent cognitive development, babies don't yet have memories to guide their interactions with the environment. If a baby is hungry, wet, sick, or tired, crying ensues. If a baby is well fed, warm, healthy, and well rested, you'll likely see big smiles and hear soft cooing. In this respect, babies' expressions reflect their immediate experience, unmediated by thinking or judging. From a baby's perspective, what happened in the past is over. A hungry baby is hungry even if he just ate. A tired baby is tired even if she slept through the night. And babies have little appreciation of the future. For example, as every parent knows, a plaintive "Wait a minute!" does little to soothe a crying baby who's sitting in a cold, wet diaper.

Given these mini mindfulness masters' apparent sagacity, here are a few tips on how to apply their teachings. They have much to teach us, even if they can't talk.

- Be with your pet or child. Spend some time following your mini mindfulness master's lead. This might simply mean lying next to your cat, nuzzling your dog, or gazing at your infant. See if you can get in touch with some of the sensual aspects of the present moment your pet or baby might be experiencing (for example, temperature, sound, lightness or darkness, and so on).

- Watch how your mini mindfulness master interacts with the present moment. Does your pet or baby seem to be experiencing something pleasant, unpleasant, or neutral? What behaviors or expressions do you notice that lead you to this conclusion? What is your own experience of this moment? Are you having a similar reaction or a completely different one? To what degree does what's going through your mind influence your experience, as opposed to what's actually happening in the world around you?

- Ask yourself, "What would Winston [or whatever your mini mindfulness master is called] do?" How would your pet or infant respond to this situation? You might anticipate reactions like purring, barking, crying, or tail wagging. Alternatively, you might expect a cocked ear or nonplussed acknowledgment. The idea isn't to embody or mimic this reaction (can you imagine growling in a crowded restaurant?) but simply to consider a different response from your usual automatic programming. If the image of your pet or baby's reaction merely brings a smile to your face, all the better.

- Notice how your mini mindfulness master's actions push your buttons. While pets and babies might be free from judging and striving, we're not. So the cat that "decides" to vomit while you're running late will likely spark feelings of anger and contempt rather than compassion. Try to bring awareness to how and when your emotions get triggered when your pet or infant behaves in ways you dislike. Some Zen parables recount how disciples became enlightened after being hit on the head or slapped in the face by the top priest. So maybe you're just one spit-up encounter away from achieving nirvana yourself!

Change Your Brain,
Change Your Roommate

Living in the city usually means living in smaller spaces. Given the expense of real estate relative to suburban and rural areas, we simply get "less bang for the buck" when it comes to square footage. To reduce expenses—or to share a life with someone we love—we end up living with others, typically roommates or a romantic partner. As a result, we're often in fairly cramped quarters as we struggle to carve out some personal space and share household responsibilities.

This kind of crowded living isn't easy. In fact, it's inherently stressful. Research shows that animals like rats and monkeys turn against each other when given too little space to live in (Calhoun 1962). Fortunately, it doesn't get to the point where we're gnawing on our roommates or hurling feces, but we do get stressed and irritable, and tend to act out in more humanlike ways. We "forget" to take out the trash or decide to wash only our own dishes. We ruminate about the ways our roommates or partners aren't doing their "fair share" to maintain the household. *I walk the dog, pay the bills, and go grocery shopping, while he can't even put away his coat,* we think.

As we get progressively more bitter and resentful, we're more likely to act out in unhealthy ways, perhaps by becoming argumentative and making snarky, passive-aggressive comments. We decide unilaterally to change our household responsibilities and just focus on doing things for ourselves. For example, we might decide to buy only the food *we* like.

In such circumstances, we clearly feel miserable. With our negative thoughts and retaliatory actions, we ruin the present moment. That glass a roommate abandoned on the kitchen table, complete with sour, stale milk, isn't as noxious as we make it out to be. We can promptly dispose of smelly milk. It's the perceived disrespect and lack of consideration that are more troubling. Through our judgments, we perpetuate our own dissatisfaction—it's our own fault we feel bad! Sure, the glass might be a catalyst, but the recrimination and perceived insult is what actually makes us feel angry and disappointed.

If you've had these kinds of experiences with your roommate or partner, you clearly need to approach the situation a little differently:

1. Become aware of what's going through your mind. What are you telling yourself about what's happening right now?

2. Consider whether or not a problem exists in this present moment. What, if anything, is wrong *right now*? Does the dog need to be walked? Do the dishes need to be washed? Do you need to eat dinner?

3. Accept that the situation is as it is. Telling yourself it "should" or "shouldn't" be this way makes it difficult to reach any constructive solution.

4. Objectively consider the problem in terms of specific behaviors. What action can you take—or try to get your roommate or partner to take—to solve the problem? Be aware of when you use judgmental language. Wanting your partner or roommate to be "more respectful" is a nice goal, but it's also too ambiguous. What do you mean by "more respectful" or whatever judgmental language you're using? See if you can articulate in behavioral terms what you would like.

If none of these strategies works, you might simply need some time alone. Research shows that we find overcrowding stressful because of a lack of desired privacy (Ramsden 2009). So maybe the dissatisfaction you feel while talking with your roommate or partner comes from doing so at a time when you would rather be alone. In such circumstances, discuss your need for more solitude and see what arrangements you can make. Though initiating this conversation might be awkward at first, it prevents future arguments and helps you feel more relaxed at home.

Talkin' Trash

Given the density of urban areas, it's not surprising that cities generate a lot of trash. According to information available at their respective sanitation departments, the cities of New York, Los Angeles, and Chicago (the three most populous U.S. cities) generate over twenty-one thousand tons of garbage daily. That's a lot of waste! Yet somehow, we don't find ourselves overwhelmed with filth. The reason, of course, is that thousands of people are responsible for removing and disposing of our garbage. Whether we bid good-bye to our trash at the wastebasket, garbage chute, or curb, many other people take it from there.

When the city's sanitation department is working well, it lulls us into a mindless complacency. We throw something away, and it soon "disappears." We don't have to concern ourselves with personally taking trash to the nearest landfill. But when the system breaks down and our garbage starts piling up too close to home (or work), we're suddenly aware of trash in a way we weren't before. We're quick to get upset or angry, even though we likely weren't particularly grateful when things worked smoothly. Based on his personal experience, the Zen monk Thich Nhat Hanh (1991) once remarked that a "non-toothache" is a pleasant experience. Similarly, we all can probably agree that having no problem with garbage collection is also a nice experience.

In this spirit, if trash pickup is important to you and your daily life, consider trying one of the following practices:

- Express your appreciation or gratitude for the people who remove the trash. Perhaps extend a blessing to the sanitation workers as they come down the block, or say thanks to your building superintendent. At the very least, maybe you can refrain from honking your horn when the garbage truck temporarily blocks your car.

- Recognize that someone else will literally be left "holding the bag" when you discard something. To reduce this person's risk of getting either injured or too messy, try to wrap broken glass securely and pour liquids down the drain before tossing the container. Consider how you would want others to dispose of garbage if *you* were responsible for carrying it away.

- Bring awareness to the process of discarding things by slowly placing trash in the garbage can rather than tossing it in. Notice what you're throwing away. If it seems appropriate, consider other uses for this item or other ways to dispose of it.

- Ask yourself, "Do I want to reduce the amount of garbage I generate?" If so, how important is this goal to you, and how much time and energy can you devote to it? Having many pressures, we need to thoughtfully consider our priorities. What you do to "reduce, reuse, and recycle" likely isn't what your neighbor does. But the question isn't about your neighbor's actions but, rather, the degree to which your own actions fit your values.

- Think about the various ways to reduce your trash. Donate or sell items, such as appliances, clothing, and furniture, through www.craigslist.org, www.freecycle.org, or a local LISTSERV. Also, many cities have a thriving "leave and take" system where people leave unwanted items on their stoops or curbs for passersby to take freely! Personally, I'm convinced that some enterprising people could furnish a whole apartment this way.

  As to recycling, leave yourself reminders to recycle, buy special recycling bins, and carry used bottles until you find a recycling bin (rather than throw them in a garbage can).

- Encourage others to recycle properly. Ask your favorite restaurants and take-out joints what happens to customers' bottles and cans. If they already recycle these items properly, thank them for their efforts. If not, encourage them to do so. Such a conversation need not be hostile or confrontational; a simple request or expression of the personal importance you place on recycling can suffice.

- Consider composting. Much of the food waste we generate can be composted into fertilizer. Even if you don't have access to a yard where you can have a compost bin, you have several other options. Often, you can bring vegetable scraps, coffee grounds, and other compostable products to your local farmers market, community garden, or food co-op. In between visits, you can keep these items in a compost pail or bag stored in the freezer. If you want to do the composting yourself, you can investigate *vermicomposting*, composting with worms. The worms live happily in your closet or under your desk, and subsist entirely on whatever fruit and vegetable scraps you would normally throw away.

- Notice the proliferation of flyers, newspapers, restaurant menus, and the like around your home or workplace. We often get bombarded by leaflets left on the doorstep or wedged into some space near the entryway. Be cognizant of what happens to these materials. Are they thrown into the trash? Does someone take and read them? Are they left outside, only to get blown into the street? If you don't want to receive such materials, consider putting up a sign or registering a complaint with the city. You can find other suggestions online about getting fewer of such unwanted advertisements.

All of these options involve becoming more aware of what you discard and the attitude you bring to the process. Changing your perspective and your waste-making behavior might introduce a better spirit and environment to your city.

Apartment Envy

For better or worse, we often compare ourselves to others, and become dissatisfied if we don't quite measure up. So-and-so has a better job, car, partner, or whatever. Researchers suggest that our tendency to make social comparisons serves an evolutionary function and that we are particularly sensitive to instances where we seem disadvantaged (Hill and Buss 2008).

In the city, a special kind of envy develops: apartment envy. Maybe you've found yourself coveting your friend's walk-in closet, dishwasher, parking spot, or incredibly low rent (or mortgage). Whatever the specifics, we're never quite satisfied with where we live, and there's ample opportunity to want what someone else has. Our reasons for envying others' homes are related to the intersection of three factors: First, the density of urban areas ensures that we're regularly reminded of people who live better than we do. These reminders come in the form of billboards, real estate ads in the newspaper, and ornate buildings. This direct experience is more unsettling for us than indirect comparisons based on, say, watching a TV show about someone's home (Alicke and Zell 2008). Second, the city's high cost of living necessarily requires us to make trade-offs in terms of location, size, and amenities. We are also limited in our ability to modify our homes; we can't just add another room if we live in an apartment, for example. Finally, there are few ways of assessing social standing in the city, compared to the suburbs or rural areas. We don't all have cars, boats, lawns, and so on, but most of us have a place to live. So our abodes take on particular significance for us.

You're likely familiar with how and when we tend to make these comparisons. At parties, for example, it's almost de rigueur to discuss each other's living spaces. We complain about noisy neighbors, lack of space, parking difficulties, insufficient interior light, unreasonable condo boards, long commutes, nonexistent outdoor space, or poor school districts. Whenever we visit friends who have just moved into a new space, we unconsciously compare their spaces to our own, noting the ways they have it better than us, or finding ways to disparage their places, thus preserving our own "apartmental" self-esteem.

You might even know people—not you, of course—who make a hobby of looking for a new and better apartment. Poring through the real estate section of the newspaper or Craigslist (www.craigs list.org), they spend much of their free time seeking the perfect place to live. However, as we all know, no place is ever perfect. There's always something less than ideal. And as our circumstances change over time, what was once "perfect" can become less so very quickly. All it takes is a yappy puppy next door to disrupt your personal Eden.

The problem in these circumstances isn't what you might normally think. Most likely, it's not that your place is too small, noisy, far, or whatever you think is wrong with it. Thus, your solution—

moving to a new apartment—is doomed to fail. The real problem is your comparative mind-set. You see—or imagine—another apartment that you decide is better than yours in significant ways. The comparison not only leads to feelings of envy and dissatisfaction, but also potentially prevents you from investing the time and energy in making your place as nice as it can be. If you're busy meeting with real estate brokers, you're not finding ways to improve your current home.

"But what if I really *do* need to move?" you might ask. Great question. You might indeed need to move to a different place. But the answer lies in looking objectively at your own needs and circumstances, not in comparing your apartment to someone else's.

To overcome apartment envy (or decide whether or not to move), look for ways to accept where you are—literally; that is, accept that you currently live in this particular apartment and neighborhood. It might not be perfect (indeed, no moment ever is), but it's what you have. Paradoxically, by bringing your attention back to your own living space and accepting it, you might discover changes you can and do wish to make. Like mindfully changing your meditation posture when you become uncomfortable, such an attitude helps you make judicious choices in nonreactive ways. Imagining yourself having to live in this apartment forever—as opposed to imagining a much better place—helps you take better ownership of the space (and maybe even improve it). Often the first step to acceptance is imagining or realizing that your situation may never change. After the anger and disappointment subside, you'll be better able to actually live where you are. Alternatively, you might realize you do indeed need to move, but now your decision comes from a place of objectivity rather than emotional reactivity.

Practice-wise, if you're still stuck envying someone else's home, here are some ways to mindfully experience what you have:

- Choose a part of your home that you particularly dislike, and sit there in silence for ten minutes. Find something there you can appreciate, and sit with that sense of appreciation for a moment. How do you feel when you are in this place? Notice your emotions, thoughts, and sensations as you sit there, but don't get hooked by them. Just notice them and let them drift away.

- Find a dissatisfying area of your home, one that isn't quite what it could or should be. Taking a step back, ask yourself, "What's wrong with this?" Notice what judgments come to mind, especially ones that compare this space to others. Consider this area of your home on its own merits. How could you describe it objectively? For example, you might describe a closet that's "too small" or "useless" as being three feet wide, two feet deep, and seven-and-a-half feet high. Given this objective description, can you see a way to compensate for whatever you think is wrong?

Spot Cleaning

Typically, we do our best to keep our living spaces clean and neat. We attend to housekeeping chores regularly or find someone else (such as a roommate, partner, or cleaning service) to do it for us. Because our living spaces can be relatively small, we often can't neglect something dirty or untidy for very long. For example, living in a studio apartment means your kitchen, living room, dining room, and bedroom are all the same room. So a sink full of dirty dishes can create a nasty odor that disturbs your guests or your sleep. In these smaller spaces, we can't easily avoid encountering a mess, or relegate it to a particular area of our homes.

Given our limited living spaces, we need to be a little more attentive to basic issues of cleanliness and tidiness. Of course, housekeeping isn't something we typically relish. It's a chore we try to get over with as quickly as possible. However, through mindfulness, we can approach this experience differently. Jon Kabat-Zinn has noted, for example, that moving our hands rhythmically in warm water can be a pleasant sensory experience for us, once we stop negatively associating this act with doing the dishes (Kabat-Zinn 1994). Indeed, we can better enjoy many of the actions involved in cleaning by becoming aware of what we're actually doing and experiencing. While cleaning the bathtub or toilet, notice how the color changes from a mildew-tinged gray or brown to something shinier and more representative of the underlying tile or porcelain. While vacuuming, feel the handle's subtle vibration and hear the crinkly slurp of dirt getting sucked into the bag. While dusting, turn your attention to the feel of the cloth in your hand or the texture of the surface you're cleaning. When we focus on our immediate sensory experience, these activities aren't unpleasant. It's the dread and reluctance we bring to these tasks that make them undesirable and off-putting. So the next time you prepare to clean your home, try some of these approaches:

- Select one area to clean thoroughly and slowly. Perhaps focus on your bedroom, bathroom, or living room. Looking at this room, how would you objectively describe whatever seems dirty or messy? If you had to give someone very specific instructions on what needs to be done, what would you say? Simply telling yourself (or someone else) "Clean up this mess" leaves room for confusion about priorities and even where to begin. You could spend considerable time dusting, for example, while the clothes remain strewn all over the floor.

- Break down an overwhelming task into smaller steps. If something is really dirty or cluttered, our minds tell us it's "too much" to do, which leads us to feel overwhelmed and to avoid cleaning at all. Notice whether you feel intimidated while approaching a particular chore. Maybe you think it will require a lot of time or energy, for example. Cognizant of your reactions and resistance, decide to do just a small part of whatever's necessary. If you have a sink full of dishes, try washing only one or two of them. If the bathtub needs scrubbing, do just one side.

- Slow down your cleaning, and practice mindfulness. As suggested earlier, sometimes you can find quite pleasant ways to connect with the sensory experience of cleaning. Also, try using this time as an opportunity to check in with your body. Notice your movements and bodily sensations as you clean. Try observing your posture as you stand there doing dishes, or feel your arm's extension and contraction as you vacuum. Further, if you use your nondominant hand, you'll naturally focus more on your bodily feelings due to the inherent awkwardness.

Though doing household chores mindfully won't make them exciting, you can discover some enjoyable moments—or at least, ones you don't resent—while cleaning. You also might be surprised to discover that you're less likely to put off what needs to be done. Of course, once you're finished, be sure to take a few moments to focus on your breathing and revel in the fresh scent of your clean home.

Thanks for the Noise, Neighbor!

Because of the density of urban areas, many of us live in close proximity to others. Houses are spaced closely together, or even touching each other, as in the case of row houses and brownstones. In apartment buildings, people literally live on top of each other. Ceilings, walls, and floors delineate your personal space, which makes it harder to perceive just how close—literally—you are to your neighbors. In fact, if you're both leaning against the same wall (albeit on opposite sides, obviously), you're probably less than six inches apart!

Because of this proximity, what happens in our neighbors' apartments more easily affects us. If our neighbors burn a cake, we smell it. If they get into a loud argument, we hear it. If they throw a raucous party, we feel their music shake our floors, windows, and walls. More catastrophic events adversely affect us too. A fire or vermin in the house next door can damage or infest our homes. Similarly, burst pipes and an overflowing toilet in the upstairs apartment can make it rain in your living room. Not surprisingly, it's easy to get annoyed, angry, and even vengeful at such times.

Compassion, kindness, gratitude? All the states of being we strive to cultivate in our lives can go out the window.

Often, we get stuck in blaming our neighbors for disturbing our peace and harmony. We consider their actions to be inconsiderate or even purposefully harmful. While confrontations can escalate to the point where neighbors are consciously feuding with each other, it's usually something more benign at the beginning. The toddler running around upstairs is playing around—not trying to disrupt our work or meditation practice. And the child's caregivers are not encouraging or condoning the behavior simply to upset us. Maintaining such negative judgments merely perpetuates destructive emotions (such as anger or hatred), making it more difficult to negotiate a successful resolution.

So what do we do? When we're angry and disturbed by our neighbors, how can we reconnect with the positive emotions toward others that we strive to elicit in more peaceful moments? And how do we get along better with our neighbors, especially when they're disturbing us?

- Don't assume your neighbors know what you can hear in your house or apartment. Often, our negative reactions are based on the assumption that they are doing something wrong to us. But almost always, our neighbors' actions result from what's going on in their own homes, not ours. This perspective suggests it might be beneficial to let the neighbors know what we're experiencing in our homes and allow them to make some adjustments in their behavior.

- Similarly, don't assume you know what's happening in your neighbors' homes. A visiting house sitter or a lost or malfunctioning remote could be causing the very loud TV. Or your neighbors might have turned up the volume to drown out a loud argument, compensate for hearing impairment, or try out some new stereo speakers. As you can see, none of these explanations has anything to do with you or your home, so don't take their actions personally.

- Politely and respectfully discuss the disturbance with your neighbors. Explain objectively how their actions, noise, and so on affect the environment in your own home. Invite them to provide feedback about you as a neighbor. Living close to each other necessarily requires us to exercise mutual respect and consideration. We can't just ask for concessions and accommodations; we have to be willing to make similar adjustments in our own lives in the interest of preserving and improving our relationships with others.

- Invite yourself to be the neighbor you would love to have. Who would be your ideal neighbor? Would you like someone who's friendly, generous, and considerate or someone who's aloof, possessive, and critical? Ultimately, you can't control your neighbors' actions, but you can control your own behavior. Instead of getting caught up in feeling disrespected, why not consider how you can change to become more considerate, accepting, and compassionate toward your noisy neighbor? Though it might take a while to improve an already strained relationship, exploring these issues might help you feel a little better now. And with repeated practice, your neighbor might eventually come around too.

Chairman Meow Is *So* Soft

We love our pets. We lavish them with attention and treats as they provide us with unconditional love and support. They become vital family members, and the next thing you know, we're discussing them at dinner parties as if they were our children. If we're not careful, though, we can forget how much they mean to us. We get caught up in the excitement and hassle of city life by going out more often or working later, and don't value our pets as much as we did initially. We might even start focusing on the negative aspects of having them around, like having to pay expensive veterinary bills, walk them outside in freezing weather, and clean up hair balls. Even nice quality time snuggling on the couch can quickly degenerate into something less enjoyable as we push them away, recalling something horrible they did earlier in the day, like peeing on the floor. If we start feeling less connected to our pets, the solution isn't to spend even less time with them. Buying more hours of doggy day care or a new scratching post won't make us enjoy being with our pets again. It might assuage our guilt temporarily or help us compensate for being unavailable for a little while, but it's not a long-term solution.

Given these considerations, why not spend some time with your furry (scaly, feathery, or whatever) loved one? Research focused on our interactions with cats and dogs shows that having pets improves our own physical and mental health (Giaquinto and Valentini 2009). For example, petting a dog can actually lower your blood pressure (Vormbrock and Grossberg 1988). So, even for your own health, it helps to reconnect with your beloved pet. If you don't have one, consider spending time with someone else's pet, like a friend's or neighbor's, or even loitering at one of those seemingly ubiquitous animal-adoption stations.

Without doing anything else, spend ten minutes simply petting, rubbing, and scratching your pet. Does this sound too easy? Well, be sure to totally focus on your pet without talking on the phone, watching TV, texting, or engaging in any other activity. Also, don't get wrapped up in looking for lumps, untangling knots, or grooming your pet in any way. The primary purpose is simply to connect with the unfolding experience through visual observation and touch. Consider what happens from two perspectives, yours and your pet's:

- What does your pet seem to like and dislike? Does your pet seem to prefer being scratched, rubbed, or petted on certain areas of the body? And does your pet prefer one kind of touch over another in these areas? What about the speed or vigorousness of the petting? Does your pet like a slow, light stroking or a rough, belly-shaking rubdown? How can you tell? What do you notice that encourages you to keep doing whatever you're doing or signals you to stop? Does your pet purr, bark, pant, whimper, coo, growl, hiss, moan, squawk, sing, bite, scratch, or walk away?

- From your own perspective, how does it feel to touch your pet's fur, coat, skin, or feathers? What do you notice as you concentrate your attention on your fingertips? Does your pet feel fluffy, wiry, scratchy, scaly, fleshy, bony, warm, or cool to your touch? How would you describe the "feel" of your pet to a stranger?

Day of Silence

One of the more powerful life experiences is to go on a silent meditation retreat. It allows you to become more aware of the sounds around—and voices within—you. Without the usual chatter, a retreat also helps you focus on your immediate experience. Typically, we seek more natural, isolated settings for this practice. Indeed, wonderful places exist all over the world where you can be with silence.

You can also create a day of silence for yourself without leaving the city. Though perhaps not as romantic as meditating by a pristine lake or desert cliff, it can be just as profound, especially since you literally bring the practice into your own home. Why not spend a whole day creating a silent retreat for yourself?

To the extent possible, create rules and a daily schedule that mirror the experience of being away from it all. Here are some of the more important considerations:

- Vow not to speak to others during the day, except in an emergency. You will maintain silence, just as if you were away on a meditation retreat.

- Inform others of your intention. Discourage people from speaking to you during this time. If you normally call your mother three times a day, tell her you won't be available during your retreat. Or perhaps invite someone to participate in the retreat with you. Especially powerful for couples living together, this option supports your mutual dedication to mindfulness and forms a special connection, allowing you to be fully present and attentive to each other—albeit wordlessly—in the same space.

- Unplug or turn off all noisy electronic distractions in your home. Don't answer the phone, watch TV, get on the computer, surf the Internet, play video games, or listen to music during this time. Obviously, the city sounds (including neighbors, roommates, pets, children, and so on) will continue, but you'll reduce the amount of noise by omitting the usual distractions.

- Schedule what you plan to do throughout the day. Typically, silent retreats have periods set aside for sitting and walking meditations. Determine the time and duration of your meditations. Depending on your familiarity with all-day retreats, perhaps plan several hour-long meditations where you alternate twenty minutes sitting with ten minutes walking.

- Select some books, chapters, verses, or poems to read. Retreats typically include periodic meetings or talks with spiritual leaders. Though you won't have the advantage of such a guide's live presence, you can find written material that provides opportunities for reflection.

- When not meditating or reading, mindfully experience whatever you do. If you're sitting on the couch, allow yourself to feel what it's like to sit. If you're walking to another room, feel how your feet make contact with the floor. You might also try some of the other mindfulness practices outlined in this part of the book, like attentively petting your dog or cat.

- Mindfully prepare and eat your meals. Ideally, try making each meal from scratch as you slowly attend to preparing each ingredient (and cooking). Try washing and drying each lettuce leaf, for example. During mealtime, focus on the food's taste in your mouth. Your tongue has different taste receptors for detecting bitter, salty, sweet, and sour flavors. These receptors are distributed on different areas of your tongue so that the same mouthful of food has a different flavor depending on its physical location. During meals, move the food around in your mouth and try to distinguish these different flavors.

- Start and end your day of silence whenever you wish. Maybe decide to practice from sunrise to sundown, or ten to two. Regardless of your selected times, maintain the boundaries; resist the urge to end prematurely. Beginning and ending your silent practice with a settling ritual, like ringing a bell or offering a compassion or gratitude prayer, also helps.

Ghost Town

Crowds, noise, and congestion contribute significantly to the stress we urbanites experience. Without these annoyances, cities actually can be quite peaceful and meditative places. Have you ever walked through the city late at night or early in the morning, when most people are asleep? A sense of calm permeates the surrounding air, despite the fact that hundreds of thousands—or even millions—of people live around you.

Unless you're an early riser or night owl, you'll have few opportunities to experience the city this way. However, it's relatively easy to imagine. Typically, such relaxation-oriented visualizations invite you to think of a walk on a beach, a hike through a forest, or a stroll through a garden. Why not try to introduce the same sense of stillness and calm by picturing yourself walking through the city or your own neighborhood? Experiencing the city this way—even in your imagination—will help you feel calmer and increase your likelihood of bringing this same relaxed attitude along when you're actually out on a walk.

Practice this meditation whenever you need a little stress relief. Maybe you are having trouble sleeping, or need to soothe yourself after a long day at work. Both circumstances are good examples of appropriate times to try this exercise.

To create a tranquil urban visualization, try to sort out all the details beforehand. Consider the following questions to get you started:

Who's around? Are you by yourself or walking with a friend? Are people in the distance, or is the area deserted, like a ghost town? Usually, it's easier to imagine that no one's around you, but you can also imagine others on the street. Ideally, they'll smile happily while passing by.

Where are you? Where will you walk? On your street, through Georgetown, along Rodeo Drive? Determining the location gives you a better sense of what it looks like. Ideally, to make it easier to bring to mind, select a place you have previously visited.

What do you notice during your walk? Elucidate the information you receive from your five senses. What do you see? Is it daytime or nighttime? What buildings and architecture do you notice? What do you smell? What's it like temperaturewise? Is it rainy or sunny?

How are you emotionally in this space? Try to imagine yourself feeling calm, secure, and peaceful. There's no point in picturing yourself scared or stressed—that's for sure! In fact, research shows that visual imagery can reduce *or* increase anxiety (Holmes and Matthews 2005). If you imagine something negative, you're more likely to feel stressed. If you imagine something positive, you're more likely to feel relaxed. Consequently, therapists often successfully use this practice to treat phobias and other anxiety disorders (Leahy 2009).

Why are you taking this walk? Is there something you want to see, like the glowing neon lights of Times Square or the rippling shore of Lake Michigan? Perhaps you simply want to get a breath of fresh air? Be sure to include this experience in your visualization.

If you enjoy this meditation, try setting aside time in the early morning or late evening for an actual walk through the city. Remaining alert for any safety concerns, try strolling slowly and mindfully down the sidewalk while basking in the city's twilight glow. Notice how it feels to be in this space, as well as whatever judgments come to mind. You might find that the actual experience is better than you imagined.

At Play

Exercising Acceptance

We spend a lot of time exercising or thinking about exercise. Every day, we're bombarded by reminders to work out and take care of our bodies. Some of us establish exercise regimens, regularly going to the gym, yoga studio, or martial arts center. Others set particular goals for athletic achievement, like running a marathon, and train accordingly. Unable to set aside consistent blocks of time for exercise, many of us try to incorporate more physical activity into our daily lives by taking the stairs instead of the elevator, or getting off the subway or bus a stop early and walking the rest of the way.

Regardless of what we do for exercise, we all have particular attitudes about it, especially its duration and intensity. But usually our judgments are pretty negative. When was the last time you heard a friend or family member complain about doing enough or even too much exercise? Have you *ever* heard someone voice these thoughts? Instead, people are more likely to dwell on what they're not doing, or feel bad about how poorly they're performing. Of course, it's all relative: one person feels guilty about being unable to make the time to run more than once a week, while another feels disappointed about being unable to break a six-minute mile.

Our tendency to berate ourselves about exercise has one of three unfortunate consequences: we lose motivation and stop exercising; we push ourselves too far beyond our capabilities, thus inviting injury; or we continue to do what we're doing while feeling miserable about it. None of these options is particularly appealing, is it? Fortunately, once we recognize the negative impact of our attitudes about exercise, we can work on cultivating a different relationship with what we're doing, one that's more grateful and accepting. Here are four tips on cultivating such acceptance:

- Describe what you do for exercise in concrete terms, without judging or evaluating. If you run twice a week, you're running twice a week. It's as simple as that. It doesn't make you a bad or good person; it just is what it is. If you can't do a headstand in yoga, you can't do a headstand. If you can, you can. Neither scenario makes you worthless or marvelous.

- Free yourself from comparisons to others. Often, we devalue our workouts because somebody's always faster, stronger, or more skillful than we are. Or we compare ourselves in the now to ourselves in the past, when we were much more athletic, slim, and fit. Though maintaining these kinds of comparisons can motivate people who are fairly competitive, they generally make the rest of us feel miserable. Doing so also increases your likelihood of pushing yourself beyond your limits in ways that might cause damage or injuries. You might add too much weight to the bench press or strain yourself during a yoga pose, just to placate your inner critic.

- Appreciate and be grateful for what you can do and have done. Being able to exercise at all suggests having a body that's capable of moving and helping us get through our daily lives. Thinking about exercising without acting on it also reflects a potentially important value for you—physical health—which helps you determine your schedule and priorities. In mindfulness-based stress reduction (MBSR), a program designed to help people with chronic pain, one of the more powerful exercises is a body scan in which participants slowly and systematically observe what's happening in each part of the body (starting with the toes) (Kabat-Zinn 1990). Not surprisingly, with this perspective, people realize that many parts of the body feel fine and work well. Similarly, for our own exercise routines, it feels better to acknowledge what's working than to dwell on what's wrong.

- Accept your injuries. When we move, we're also more likely to get injured; it's a risk inherent in any activity. Even when walking down the street (especially while chewing gum), we're at risk of falling or twisting an ankle. And over time, we can accumulate injuries that turn into chronic conditions if we rush the healing process. As a result, we need to simply accept our own limitations and pain. It might not be fair or what you want, but it's how things are. Railing against your injuries or pushing yourself in painful ways simply aggravates your condition, delays your recovery, and worsens your pain, thus limiting your activities in the future. Sure, it isn't fair that you have this injury. But most likely, there's *something* you can do physically. Maybe it's not specifically what you want, but perhaps it reflects the value you place on health, which underscores your commitment to exercise in the first place.

Can You Smell That?

Ah, cities! The wonderful sights, sounds, and smells! *Smells?* What's so nice about the smells? We've got smog, litter, trash, and dog poop! What smells good about that?

Nothing, really. Cities usually don't smell very nice. Admittedly, country living is no picnic either; ever driven near a chicken farm? Yet, like other aspects of urban living, unpleasant smells can be a wake-up call to mindfulness—a kind of spiritual smelling salts, if you will.

When we find ourselves smelling something "bad" or rotten, we can notice our revulsion and distaste. We can also choose to remove ourselves from that particular place in hope of finding something nicer a little farther away. Being mindful and accepting the present moment doesn't mean you need to resign yourself to putting up with something bad if you can change it. If you're standing really close to a pile of garbage and it smells bad, move. No special dignity or award lies in tolerating an unpleasant situation that you can easily change. The difference is in the attitude you bring to the situation. If you notice a distasteful smell and simply move—wonderful! But it's not so helpful to get preoccupied with the smell's source, curse the city's lack of cleanliness, and start remembering all of the rotten smells you've ever experienced.

Of course, in addition to the city's "bad" smells, we can easily find pleasant ones too, like the aroma of baking bread wafting outside bakeries and bagel shops. Florist shops, fruit stands, farmers markets, cafés, perfumeries, candle stores, and body-care shops all provide an opportunity to smell something nice. In New York, freshly cut flowers typically line the fronts of bodegas. Usually, a tarp hangs down from the storefront to protect them from direct sunlight, plus it serves to keep the wonderful scents of the roses, lilies, and hyacinths concentrated in the small space. Aaah, spending a few moments immersed in the sweet, honey-like aromas is a delightful way to recharge before rushing to your next appointment.

A Walk In the Park

For centuries, societies and cultures worldwide have expressed the need to "get away from it all." Whether by going on a religious pilgrimage or vacationing on Martha's Vineyard, people seek experiences outside their day-to-day environments. For us urbanites, this usually means some combination of hiking in the country, skiing in the mountains, camping in the woods, swimming at the beach, or simply picnicking in the local park. If we have a little money to spend, this excursion can involve touring wine country, attending a yoga retreat, or relaxing at a spa. Intuitively, we're drawn to natural settings, and research demonstrates that being in nature is associated with promoting health and well-being (Hartig et al. 2003). But why?

About twenty years ago, Stephen and Rachel Kaplan (no relation to the author) proposed a theory of why we benefit more psychologically and physiologically from being in nature than in cities. Their *attention restoration theory* suggests that environments requiring directed, sustained attention, like living in chaotic urban areas, eventually drain our mental resources, leaving us feeling tired and less able to manage surrounding uncertainty and stress (Kaplan and Kaplan 1989). Natural settings, which require only indirect attention, thus provide an opportunity to recharge our mental batteries.

Consider an example comparing hiking in the mountains with walking down a busy street. Generally, hiking doesn't require a focused, top-down kind of attention. We get enjoyment from the rich sensory environment of sounds, smells, and sights, but nothing *demands* our attention. We don't focus on a specific tree or bird-call, but rather attend to the symphony-like integration of sensory stimuli. In contrast, walking down a busy street requires more of both our direct and indirect attention. Our indirect attention is consumed by dramatic stimuli, like sirens, provocative window displays, and interesting smells. Our direct attention not only tries to suppress this competing information but also focuses on dodging oncoming pedestrians and making sure we don't step on anything too disgusting.

So, attention restoration theory suggests that one reason we feel better in nature is that it requires less attention (Kaplan 1995). By not demanding such an intense use of our directed attention, being in nature allows us to rest and recharge our attentional batteries, if you will. Previous research indeed supports the corresponding hypothesis that our attention and memory improve when we're in nature (Berto 2005). Fortunately for us city dwellers, we can get similar relief without retreating to the country.

In 2008, a group of University of Michigan researchers tested attention restoration theory by comparing a walk downtown with a walk in the park (literally) (Berman, Jonides, and Kaplan 2008). In a well-designed experiment, they discovered that both conditions helped improve participants' attention and short-term memory. However, the participants in the group that walked in the park (for about an hour) had a significantly greater improvement in ability to concentrate. They also felt better moodwise, which was unrelated to their improved attention.

So if you ever struggle with flagging attention at work or simply need a break, maybe you'll benefit from a little dose of nature. Check out the many options around you:

- Take a stroll in your local park. Be sure to venture into areas where you are more surrounded by plant life, rather than merely walk around the periphery or near a main road. Ideally, try to have as few as possible of the usual urban distractions.

- Explore the unexpected green space around you, like a rooftop garden, museum spot, florist's shop, or naturally scenic area on a local college campus.

- Check out your local botanical garden, which provides a nice opportunity to view a lot of different kinds of plants within a relatively small space.

- Theoretically, looking across an ocean or lake brings similar relief. So if you live or work near a large body of water (like in Chicago or San Francisco), spend some time looking toward the horizon. Admittedly, this might look a little bizarre to passersby. But if anyone asks, just say you're waiting for your lover to return from sea.

In all of these circumstances, try to simply be in the space and experience it mindfully. Resist the temptation to bring a book or check your phone messages. Immerse yourself as much as possible in the nature around you.

Flecks of Green

Water cascades down a vertical wall of rock, creating a muffled roar as it splashes into the pool below. Pink and purple flowers burst like fireworks. Sunlight peeks through the canopy of trees overhead, casting shadows that dance across the mottled stones underfoot. Sounds nice, huh? A bucolic retreat to nature? Not quite. What if I said you can have this pleasant experience in a small lot between office buildings in midtown Manhattan? Paley Park, a private park made available for the public, is located near the intersection of Fifth Avenue and Fifty-third Street.

Since the creation of cities, we've set aside natural areas for public use in the form of parks. Typically, these parks required that a large amount of space be dedicated for this purpose. For example, the National Mall in Washington, D.C., is over three hundred acres, San Francisco's Golden Gate Park is over a thousand acres, and San Diego's Balboa Park is about twelve hundred acres. Over the past few decades, there has been a growing movement to create smaller urban spaces dedicated to nature too. Literally sprouting all over town, these smaller parks are known by many names, including "microparks," "pocket parks," and "miniparks." Some of these parks are professionally developed (for example, Waterfall Garden in Seattle), while others reflect the actions of neighbors armed with trowels and seed packets.

Old, abandoned rail lines have also been converted into parks, providing a strip of nature through crowded urban areas. In New York, an abandoned elevated train track was reclaimed as an urban garden and dubbed the High Line. According to Friends of the High Line (personal communication), in less than six months of operation, over a million people had visited the park. In Chicago, people have organized to try to create a park along another elevated rail line, called the Bloomingdale Trail.

Rebar, an interdisciplinary collection of San Francisco artists, developed another interesting reclamation of space. In 2005, they created an art installation of a small park located literally within the confines of a parking space. Since then, Rebar's PARK(ing) Day has been celebrated annually in cities worldwide, as artists, citizens, organizations, and companies create small oases of green in parking spots. If you want to learn more, visit the Rebar website (www. rebargroup.org) or the PARK(ing) Day website (www.parkingday. org), or even join the community of people dedicated to creating these spaces (my.parkingday.org).

Whether in the form of a micropark or the temporary greening of a parking spot, these flecks of green in the city can be hard to find. They typically have a small footprint, despite their growing numbers. If you're interested in exploring new locales for contemplation, here are a few suggestions:

- Conduct an Internet search of your city or neighborhood with the terms "micropark," "vest park," "pocket park," and "minipark." You might be surprised to discover a small park tucked around the corner from your work or home.

- Visit the website of Project for Public Spaces (www.pps.org), an organization operating for over thirty years that lists "Great Public Spaces" in cities worldwide.

- Find a satellite image or bird's-eye view of the area around your home and work. From this new perspective, you might discover an open space that's hidden from view when you're on the street.

- Regularly visit blogs that reflect what's happening in your neighborhood. Local blogs reflect the word on *your* street and thus can reveal interesting green spaces in planning or development.

- Finally, be on the lookout for any vacant, overgrown lots around you. By conducting a little research on the address, you might discover some unused public space that you can convert into a small park or community garden (with a lot of help from your friends!). The land for a recently inaugurated community garden in Brooklyn, for example, was initially discovered while a local resident was trying to find a vacant lot for parking his car. The overgrown lot seemed like a perfect choice, until he discovered that it was owned by the New York City Department of Parks and Recreation. A quest for parking unearthed a new space for urban gardeners! Maybe you can find a similar undiscovered treasure in your neighborhood.

Toddler Time

Young children are very mindful beings: they're curious about their experiences, accepting of their emotions, and exquisitely attuned to what's happening in the present moment. For example, as a toddler, my oldest son showed an avid interest in pigeons. He was quick to spot them and squealed delightedly as he chased after them. After they'd flown away, he would pick up a forgotten feather, which became an object of meditation for the whole day. The rest of us either don't usually notice pigeons or judge them negatively (for example, "rats with wings"). Of these perspectives, which do you think would bring you more happiness?

It seems as if, through our contemplative practice, we're often trying to regain these childlike qualities. Though we might not want to run through flocks of birds, we certainly envy the excitement, freshness, and lack of self-consciousness of those who do. If you have children (or see them around), you can learn valuable lessons from them as they interact with you and the world around them:

- Observe what consumes a child's attention. Children have a plethora of first-time experiences as they go through the day. They readily carry the Buddhist perspective of *beginner's mind*, which refers to the ability to experience aspects of life with openness, devoid of preconceptions. Children haven't developed many of the rigid ways of thinking about the world that we adults have. Also, because they're shorter, they naturally notice things that are closer to the ground more than we do. Watching a toddler discover the many joys of playing in a fountain can help us reconnect to some of the same enjoyable sensory experiences, like feeling cool water soothe our skin on a hot day.

  But our interactions with children aren't always so beatific and happily inspiring. Sometimes we get stressed around children, such as when they have tantrums or refuse to eat dinner at the appropriate hour. These frustrating times can also serve as opportunities for mindfulness practice.

- Practice acceptance and mindful breathing whenever you start feeling angry or stressed around children. Typically, we get angry because they're not doing what we want them to do. In reality, they have exactly the same experience: we're not doing what they want either. Rather than forcefully assert what we want or threaten yet another punishment, what if we took a time-out? Take a few moments to settle down and let go of your own agenda, at least temporarily. Reengage children to empathically uncover what they want or the basis of their objections. Often, this simple act of understanding can break down resistance, facilitating a mutually satisfying compromise. For example, a sick child who refuses to take medicine and demands apple juice can, in fact, have both.

- Ask yourself what kind of parent, grandparent, or watchful adult you want to be. Like writing in wet cement, it's easy to communicate messages to children that become "concretized" as beliefs about themselves, others, and the world. Being aware of your actions and demeanor, consider what you want to communicate. Do you want to convey judgment, disapproval, or criticism or to emphasize love, kindness, and compassion? How do you embody these principles to get your message heard loud and clear? How do children respond to what you've done?

- Offer to help when you see a parent or caregiver struggling to manage a difficult situation. Rather than get embroiled in your own judgments about what's happening or ignore it entirely, see if you can lend a hand. Perhaps do this literally, for example, by lifting one end of the stroller as a child's caregiver navigates the subway-station stairs, or by holding open a door. You might also try to coax a smile from a crying child. In such circumstances, consider what kind of help you might appreciate if you were this child's caretaker.

Mindfulness Master

We love to play games. As children, we spent hours playing catch, tag, and hide-and-seek. As we grew, our games and tastes became more sophisticated. We now play organized sports, gather around board games, and challenge ourselves with puzzles like crosswords and sudoku.

Over the past thirty or so years, since the invention of the arcade video game Pong, we've become more and more avid about video games, which grow more visually appealing, realistic, and elaborate in their depictions of alternative worlds every year. Video games are also more widely available than ever. Whereas before, we needed a computer or video game console, now we play games on our phones, MP3 players, and other handheld devices.

As we get involved in playing a video game, we naturally lose contact with the world around us. Our total engrossment in the game's action doesn't allow us to be mindful. A snack consumed while playing can seemingly disappear because we don't even register that we're eating. These games provide such enticing distraction because they are inherently fun and use a powerful psychological principle of learning and behavior.

Based on the pioneering work of B. F. Skinner, *operant conditioning* is a compelling explanation of how playing video games (and gambling) can be so addictive. Essentially, this principle shows that we're more likely to perform an action when we receive a reward afterward. Furthermore, our tendency to repeat this action becomes stronger based on several factors, including receiving bigger rewards, getting them very soon after the action, and receiving them intermittently (see, for example, Skinner 1953). If we hear a satisfying "explosion" or get points whenever we "shoot" an alien, we want to shoot more aliens. Our action has been reinforced. However, if we receive the same reward for everything we do, we can become bored with it. We're also more likely to stop performing that action if we suddenly cease receiving rewards. So the secret to getting us to keep doing something is to provide rewards periodically. The possibility of scoring higher, unlocking special characters or abilities, or getting a bigger payout next time keeps us motivated to continue.

With a dash of playfulness, we can also use this same principle to promote our self-care and mindfulness practice. So, let me introduce you to the game that's captivated people all across the globe for generations: Mindfulness Master. Uncover the secrets of ancient civilizations as you challenge yourself to walk the mystical path of mindfulness. You'll need a pen and paper to record your score. Oh, you need to breathe, too. Before I introduce the rules, put down your cell phone, PDA, or handheld video game. You won't need it to play Mindfulness Master.

I. Select a period of time (such as five minutes) or discrete experience (such as walking to work) for playing this game.

2. Bring your attention and awareness to your breathing. The main goal of the game is to count how many complete breaths (inhalation and exhalation) you can follow mindfully before becoming distracted. Give yourself one point for each breath cycle.

3. Continue breathing and giving yourself points until your mind wanders away from your breathing. As soon as you stop focusing on your breath, the game is over.

4. Record your results.

5. Play as many times as you like and try to beat your score. How high can you go? Can you reach the highest level, nirvana?

This game obviously introduces some competing and striving, which isn't really consistent with mindfulness. However, it reflects your underlying intention and encourages you to unplug your devices and focus on your breathing, which cultivates concentration and awareness. Playfully engaging in the present like this helps you find encouraging ways to cultivate and support your own practice, especially whenever your interest and commitment fade.

You See 'Em, Museum!

Every city has at least one art museum and thus a wonderful opportunity for getting a little dose of culture. Many cities have more than just one. The Dallas–Fort Worth area has over twenty prominent art museums and art-related cultural centers, for example. Despite the plethora of opportunities, evidence suggests that people actually spend very little time appreciating exhibits and artwork. Beverly Serrell (1997) discovered that visitors usually spend less than twenty minutes in special exhibitions. A *New York Times* correspondent more recently decried how visitors to the Louvre spend more time snapping photos than actually looking at the paintings (Kimmelman 2009). Given art's visually stimulating nature, museums provide inspiring opportunities for mindfulness practice, and even instill a kind of relaxation similar to being in nature (Kaplan, Bardwell, and Slakter 1993). If you're willing to spend a little more time and energy appreciating what your museum has to offer, here are some suggestions:

- Bring a sketchbook and charcoal, pastels, or colored pencils, and spend some time drawing a painting or other artwork. For at least twenty minutes, focus on drawing what you really see. Often, our drawings are based on our mental representation of something rather than how it actually looks; for example, even if sunlight causes color and shadow changes, we might draw something as though evenly lit. So, sit down and spend some time drawing the colors, forms, and shapes you actually see, making your drawing as realistic as possible. If you're "not an artist," notice the judgments that arise as you consider doing this activity.

- Take a mental photograph. Visually take in all a particular artwork's details, and then close your eyes. See if you can re-create or envision the artwork in your mind's eye.

- Change your position and perspective relative to an artwork. What changes when you move closer or farther away? Is your attention drawn to different aspects of the work? Where do you start seeing the whole piece, rather than merely specific parts of it?

- Reconsider the masterpieces. Many works of art are universally recognized as historical treasures, like Michelangelo's *David*, da Vinci's *Mona Lisa*, and Monet's *Water Lilies*. But why? When you see such a work, look at it with "beginner's eyes." What do you notice? How do you feel?

- Wander and get lost among the artwork, rather than race to particular pieces. Stroll from room to room, drawn by the visual appeal of whatever attracts you.

- Become aware of how it feels to be in a particular space. Considerable thought and planning go into the design of museums and exhibits. Curators pay particular attention to the aesthetics of the space. Notice the architecture, interior design, lighting, and arrangement of art around you.

While this chapter focused on art museums, you can apply many of these practices to art galleries and other kinds of museums. A science museum, for example, has many interactive displays that invite experimentation. You might notice the degree of force you exert while interacting with an exhibit on magnetism or suction. Natural history museums have engaging dioramas of wildlife and indigenous peoples that you can mindfully observe. Regardless of the particular museum, give yourself permission to slowly appreciate whatever's present. Don't concern yourself with making it educational; we're more likely to go to museums as an "escape" than a learning experience (Slater 2007). If you follow some of these suggestions, you probably won't get to see all the museum's exhibits: mindfulness takes time. While you might not see everything, the alternative—rushing through the museum—pretty much ensures that you won't *really* see *anything.*

The Clothes Make the City, Man

A fun aspect of city living is shopping, especially for clothes. You can find many beautiful and stylish outfits at department stores, thrift shops, discount chains, consignment stores, and boutiques. Sample sales also crop up in previously vacant storefronts, offering ephemeral chances to find something special. Budding designers and artists offer their latest creations in flea markets and sidewalk stands.

Given all of these options, it's easy for us to get "wanty" (despite our lack of closet space). We see something and we want it. Sometimes, we simply get swept up in the allure and fantasy of our purchases. We imagine ourselves wearing them to an important function or a "night on the town." Sometimes we simply go for the label, whether based on personal experience (like knowing this brand usually fits well) or what we associate with the designer's name. In fact, designer clothing usually has extra cachet: its presumed style, exclusivity, and high price make us want it more!

At such times, we can get carried away by the moment and make impulse purchases. I imagine each of us can point to a few things in the closet that we bought with much fanfare and now regret. What seemed so desirable in the past, we'd now like to give away. This process is nothing new; in fact, it's related to one of the central tenets of Buddhism: desire causes suffering. Typically, this refers to the desire for things to be unlike how they actually are. In this case, we initially were dissatisfied by not having this item of clothing, so we bought it. And a little while later, we feel unhappy because we wish we had something else instead.

With a little self-reflection, we can become aware of the personal factors that influence our decision to buy something. Without becoming mindful of our own habits and motivations, we're more likely to buy things we don't really need or want. We also can overspend or buy things carelessly. More subtle influences are at work as well. Research into consumer psychology reveals many factors that influence our decision to buy something; for example, if something is touchable, on sale, and not immediately obvious (that is, we "discover" it), we're more likely to buy it (Underhill 1999).

To reduce the influence of these conscious and unconscious factors, it can help to introduce a little awareness to your shopping decisions. Next time you look for clothes, consider these questions:

What do I need? Before you go shopping, look in your closet. Based on what you have, what do you need? Given your penchant for buying shirts, you might notice you need pants instead. Thus, you can focus specifically on getting pants without wandering over to the shirts section of the store.

What values, if any, do I want my purchasing decisions to reflect? If you buy organic food, for example, you might look for clothes made with organically grown materials. Or you might decide it's important to buy stylish, trendsetting, well-made, or bargain clothes. Whatever principles you choose, be sure to uphold them when you shop.

Does this fit me comfortably? Too often, we buy clothes that don't fit. We tell ourselves it's a good deal or promise to lose weight. And typically, we rarely wear what we bought, precisely because it doesn't fit well. Accept the reality of how it feels on your body. If it's too tight or too loose, that's too bad.

What catches my eye and why? See what clothes look appealing to you based on their actual appearance and fit. Avoid looking for designer clothing first, unless you know you like the collection. Try to see each outfit from a fresh perspective, untainted by its pedigree.

How much would I pay for this? Obviously, this question carries more weight if you ask it before you look at the price tag. Determining how much something is worth to you puts the purchase on your terms. If the price is within your range, go ahead and buy it. If not, seriously consider the purchase. Notice whether your mind tries to justify the extra expense and how.

With these questions, we can approach our spending more mindfully, buying outfits that fit our bodies and budgets. We can also be more purposeful in our purchases once we understand our values.

Mindful Online Dating

Online dating is a very efficient and convenient way to meet people. You can describe whom you'd like to date, cruise profiles, and screen potential dates by e-mail, online chat, text, and phone before actually meeting in person. You can also consider and develop criteria for your ideal partner. If you want to meet only people who live in your zip code, you can screen out everyone else. If it's vitally important to be with someone who, like you, loves pugs, you can find that type of person too. And you can do all of this without even leaving your home!

A consequence of this process is spending an awful lot of "alone time" writing (and updating) your profile, selecting the best photo of yourself, and poring through everyone else's profile. During this time, you're vulnerable to two very unmindful phenomena: stewing in others' opinions about you and concocting fantasies about others. In both situations, exercising your judgmental mind can make you easily fall prey to disastrous dating experiences.

Developing your dating profile requires you to articulate who you think you are. Typically, this conjures both positive and negative views of yourself. You might easily identify all of your good qualities, like being honest or having a healthy head of hair. Or you might feel bad about who you are, particularly relative to someone else or an idealized version of yourself. For example, "I'm too fat," "I'm not successful," and "I'm not as funny as my friend" are all variations on the "I'm not good enough" theme. Regardless of whether your self-assessment is negative, positive, or some combination, the bottom line is that you spend considerable time and energy being distracted by opinions of yourself.

Related to this issue, you spend a lot of time thinking about whom you want to date. Maybe you're looking for a vegetarian chef or a fellow Christian. A quick search might identify plenty of suitable matches in your neighborhood. Having so many search options can actually lead you to select poorer matches as you become distracted by irrelevant details and less attentive to what you really want (Wu and Chiou 2009). In addition, it can create fantasies of how you expect or want someone else to be. Again, you're distracted from the present moment—in this case, the actual experience of being with someone.

In both situations, as you consider yourself and others as dating material, these fantasies (and they are fantasies) get concretized in a way that leads to dissatisfaction and dating disasters. If you think you're a loser, for example, you likely set your sights low, easily misperceive yourself as being rejected, and try to cover up your self-determined flaws. If you think that person with the cat photo is a freaky animal lover who can't relate to people, you might shy away from (or be attracted to) him or her. And because you're familiar with this mutually evaluative process, you make compensatory adjustments. Consequently, your profile reflects not who you truly are, but rather who you think you need to be to get who you think you want. So what do you do? You want to date, and you already paid money for the online matchmaking service. So you might as well use it—but mindfully. Here are a few questions to ponder:

1. As you imagine yourself dating, how do you feel? Excited, nervous, discouraged, triumphant?

2. Given these emotions, what do you notice yourself wanting to do? Edit your profile, conduct another search, shut down the computer, go out on another date?

3. In creating your profile, how did you describe yourself? What did you decide to share and why? Does it truly reflect your opinions of yourself? Does it include the opinions of your friends, family members, or previous partners?

4. As you read others' profiles, be aware of what you notice. Do you focus on the picture, the person's occupation? To what degree does your reaction reflect what's actually written or shown versus the judgments you've made in your head about the person?

5. Without getting too analytical, consider for a moment where these judgments originated. With curiosity and openness to whatever arises, investigate what got your mind started down this path.

6. Finally, spend a few minutes breathing mindfully before taking yourself back to the task at hand. As you reengage with the present moment through your breathing, you develop your ability to see people— yourself and others—as they truly are. Afterward, you

can return to whatever you were doing online, if it still seems appropriate. Increasing your awareness of your judgments and reactions can reaffirm your commitment to a particular action or change your course. You might decide to continue editing your profile, for instance, or to just let it be. Either way is okay.

Urban "Winefulness"

Many of us drink alcohol. The city's plentiful diversity of bars, wineshops, happy hours, and events ensures that we can always find a drink when we want one. Usually, our reasons for drinking alcoholic beverages are fairly benign, based on enjoyment of the taste or a desire to unwind (as opposed to a pathological urge to numb emotional pain). The pleasant effects of drinking come pretty soon after we start. By mindfully attuning to the experience, we can continue to enjoy a series of pleasurable moments without drinking too much. When we get disconnected from our bodily feelings, we become vulnerable to drinking excessively. We fail to notice our diminished ability to taste our drinks and don't observe the decline in our physical, mental, and social faculties. Many religious traditions eschew drinking, especially by spiritual leaders, because they consider it to interfere with awareness, purpose, and divine will. While it might be going too far for some people to consider not drinking at all, most can recall times when drinking led to some poor decision making or a nasty hangover.

Introducing mindfulness to the times when we drink can be an interesting and enriching experience. Consider some of the following activities:

- Be aware of your need or urge to drink. Ideally, drinking is enjoyable and voluntary, not compulsive and necessary. In stressful times, we're more likely to crave a drink as a quick way to feel better. However, we can also relieve stress through exercise, meditation, and diaphragmatic breathing. Mindfully observing what judgments or feelings lead us to drink can provide valuable insights into our own behavior. In fact, using mindfulness to bring attention to—without acting on—the urge to drink is a key component of relapse prevention for alcohol abuse (Marlatt and Gordon 1985).

- Drink slowly. Bring your full awareness to the taste and aroma of your drink. The taste of some beverages, like wine, beer, and whisky, changes as they further aerate and adjust to room temperature. See if you can detect any subtle changes in flavor. While a primer in tasting is beyond the focus of this chapter, it might help to know some of the characteristics associated with different drinks. Beer, for example, has flavors associated with malt (such as sweet, earthy, and caramel-like) and hops (such as crisp, bitter, and grassy).

- Notice when you start to feel buzzed or drunk. How does this feel in your body? Is it pleasurable or unsettling? If you start to feel bad, it's clearly time to stop or slow down. Similarly, if you find yourself losing the ability to taste your drink, you might be going beyond the point of a pleasant experience. Consider taking a time-out or stopping altogether, and drinking some water or club soda instead.

- Remain cognizant of your reason(s) for drinking right now to ensure that your actions are consistent with your goal(s). Sometimes, your intention to hang out with friends or watch a ballgame might be superseded by your desire for another drink. Presumably, you don't want to miss an interesting conversation or the best play of the game by standing in line at the bar.

At Work

Coffee with Milk, Sugar, and Mindfulness

In all likelihood, you drink coffee. In fact, every day, over 50 percent of Americans drink coffee (National Coffee Association 2009). What do you like in it? Cow or soy milk, or cream, or do you just take it black? Do you like coffee with sweetener or sugar? You can probably answer these questions pretty easily. You know how you order coffee and what you like to add to it. In fact, it has probably become part of your morning routine, something you tend to do mindlessly, on automatic pilot. This process of habituation can be adaptive because it allows us to dedicate our attention and mental capacity to novel stimuli and thoughtful analysis. But there are times when it screens out pleasant experiences, tastes, and sensations simply due to familiarity. Thus, chances are that if you drink coffee regularly, you rarely actually taste it. In fact, it's almost as if you stop enjoying your coffee once you figure out what you like and grow accustomed to its flavor.

It may come as a surprise, but no two cups of coffee taste exactly the same. Many factors influence the taste of coffee: its region (and farm) of origin, its roast, its blend with other beans, and the seasonal growing conditions of the coffee plants themselves. Once you've brewed a cup of coffee, many other factors come into play, too: the water, the ratio of beans to water, the grind of the coffee, its temperature, the ratio of coffee to milk, and even the precise number of sugar granules that pour into your cup. Many people have opined that the present moment is always changing, and so is your morning cup of joe.

As mentioned earlier, in Buddhism mindfulness is often associated with the concept of beginner's mind. Essentially, it involves approaching the present moment openly, as if you were experiencing it for the first time. In fact, this is actually true. You haven't experienced this precise moment before because it didn't exist. It's unfolding right before you. You have, of course, been introduced previously to many of the elements of what's happening right now. Based on your prior experiences, you know what coffee is and how you generally prefer it, which helps streamline the whole process: if you approached every liquid as a mysterious, potentially dangerous substance, it would take you a long time to drink it! However, selectively reintroducing mindfulness to your experience of drinking coffee—as if for the very first time—can be quite enjoyable and provide a nice way to reconnect with something you used to enjoy.

Coffee-Tasting Primer

I. Next time you order or make a cup of coffee, pay attention to its aroma before even taking a sip. How does it smell? Earthy, spicy, carmel-like, chocolaty, fruity?

2. Then take a sip and notice its flavor in your mouth. Be sure to allow yourself to smell the coffee as you taste it, because the aroma influences how it tastes. This means, of course, that you might need to take off the lid to invite a new flavor experience.

3. Professional coffee tasters typically take note of the flavor, body, sweetness or acidity, and aftertaste:

   a. Flavors can include some of the following, many of which mirror the aromas you initially detected: chocolate, caramel, berry, nutty, winelike, or earthy.

   b. You can describe body as how the coffee "feels" in your mouth. Is it light, heavy, or somewhere in between? Does it cling to your tongue or quickly wash away?

   c. Sweetness or acidity refers to the degree of tanginess in your brew. Does it leave you flat, or does your tongue pucker up a little?

   d. Finally, take note of the aftertaste. What's the lingering flavor of the coffee?

   e. If all this seems too complicated, try using a much simpler tasting system: yum, yuck, or meh.

4. In addition to tasting your coffee, try bringing mindful attention to the physical sensations involved in holding your cup. How does the cup feel? How hot or cold is it? Can you feel its temperature transferring to your

hands and fingertips as you hold it, and then slowly subside after you put it down?

5. Once you've enjoyed your coffee, learn its name and roast so you'll know what to buy later. Depending on the day, you might decide you're in the mood for a light, citrusy coffee or an earthy, caramel-like brew, and make your selection accordingly.

When Does Your Workday Begin and End?

At your job, you probably have a predetermined schedule. You're expected to show up at work and go home at a particular time. If you're a freelancer or consultant, you might not have designated work hours, but you're expected to produce a certain amount of work or labor an approximate number of hours. Despite these limits, you probably spend a lot more time working than you realize. Maybe you take work home or compulsively check your e-mail and voice mail for important messages. Even if you try to establish some boundaries for what you do, you probably think about work when you're trying to do something else, like sleeping or spending time with the kids.

Suppose I asked you this question: "When does your workday begin, and when does it end?" You might respond with the times you show up and leave your workplace. What if I asked, "When do you first start thinking about work each day, and when do you stop thinking about work?" Now your answer will be different. Some of you might reply that you never stop thinking about work!

What effect does thinking about work outside your workplace have on your life? In some cases, it might help you perform your job more successfully. While mulling things over at home, you might come up with better ways to deal with a difficult customer or teach a complicated subject. In other situations, you get mired in regret over something that happened in the past, or worry about what the future holds. In all of these situations, you're getting lost in your thoughts and losing contact with your immediate experience, which can lead to multitasking and an unwitting increase in stress. Further, your lack of mental presence causes you to lose the experience you could have had in the present moment. Why bother doing anything if you can't be there for it?

To practice mindfulness more effectively, you'll need to get a better handle on your thinking about work, especially when you're not working. Here are a few approaches to help you leave work at work, and thus attend mindfully to your life experiences as they develop:

- Become aware of when you first start thinking about work each day. If it's difficult to catch your thoughts about work, you might more easily perceive a shift in your emotions. For example, you might start feeling stressed, anxious, or excited about something you expect to happen that day. When you observe a change in your mood, ask yourself what just passed through your mind.

- Give yourself permission to enjoy some of the sensory pleasures associated with the start of each workday. For example, let yourself feel the warm water of the shower in lieu of planning the day's schedule. You might also decide to eat breakfast mindfully or devote 100 percent of your attention to your children once they get out of bed.

- Decide to leave work behind once you leave your workplace. If there's nothing else for you to do between now and the next time you go to work, make a mental note to let go. You might even imagine yourself shutting the door on your thoughts about work, or leaving them in a particular place for you to visit later. Like it or not, your work and these concerns will be there when you return.

- Consider setting aside some time for a morning or evening meditation (or both) to help you transition between work and home. Meditation at these times helps you recognize the degree to which thoughts of work distract you. Also, please note that your meditation need not be a formal, sit-down event. You can practice a walking meditation or select another exercise from the "Out and About" part of this book.

- Develop some rules about how much you'll work or think about work when you're not there. For example, consider never checking your work e-mail once you enter your home. Or perhaps don't answer work-related calls after midnight. Decide on something that seems like a reasonable accommodation between your job responsibilities and mental health.

- Leave reminders to yourself in places where you're likely to fall prey to thinking about work. Sticky notes can suffice, or it can be something more elaborate, like setting a bell to chime or setting your computer screen saver to change automatically at intervals. You can also set a countdown alarm on your phone, watch, or PDA to prompt a mindful pause several hours from now.

Thanks, Stapler!

To accomplish our work, we rely on many people to help us. While it's easy to recognize others' helpful contributions when they do something to help us directly, like deliver a phone message or help write a memo, it's more difficult to appreciate the assistance of people we'll never meet who have helped us tremendously through their labor.

Consider the stapler. Presumably you've had occasion to staple papers together. It's a tremendously convenient and easy way to bind pages, right? There might even be a stapler close to you right now. If so, please pick it up and examine it for a few moments. If you don't have a stapler handy, just pick up whatever random work-related object is close by.

1. Examine the stapler solely with your sense of touch (you might want to close your eyes). How heavy does it feel to you? Can you estimate its weight? Allow your

fingers to glide over its surface. Does it feel smooth or rough? How would you describe its slickness or stickiness? What about the edges? Do they feel rounded or sharp? How would you describe the stapler's surface temperature? Does it feel cool or warm? Does its temperature differ depending on where you touch it? As your fingers explore the stapler, allow yourself to notice areas of empty space and openness, where your fingers fall away from tracing its shape or outline.

2. As you examine the stapler, notice what thoughts and judgments come to mind. Whatever they are (for example, "This is silly" or "I have to make that phone call ASAP"), simply make a mental note and return your attention to this exercise.

3. Now, visually examine the stapler. What do you see? What color is it? Do you notice differences in shading? What about reflections? Can you see any light reflections or aspects of the surrounding room on its surface? Does the stapler sparkle or look dull? Can you detect any variability in these attributes across its surface? Is there any writing on the stapler? What does it say?

4. Now, hold the stapler up to your ear (not too close) and squeeze it shut. Notice the sound the stapler makes. How long does it resonate? Is it high pitched or low pitched? Does the sound change over time?

Now that you've examined your stapler in a sensory way (we'll skip tasting and smelling it), take a couple of moments to appreciate how it connects you to others in the world. Sharing the stapler with someone else in the office is an easily identifiable example of this connection; this simple office tool also serves as an example of interdependence. Consider these questions:

- How did this stapler end up on your desk? Who put it there?

- Where was it before it came to be in front of you? Did it come from home, a supply closet, or a store?

- How was it transported there? Who helped bring it to that location?

As you trace the origins of this stapler, consider all the people who were involved in making it appear on your desk at this time and place. If you noticed earlier that the stapler was made in China or another country, you can imagine its long journey and the vast number of people who facilitated its safe arrival at your workplace. The factory workers, the delivery people, the customs agents, and many others helped deliver this simple stapler to you. If you expand this consideration further by noting all the people who helped them do their jobs (such as the workers who designed and built the factory), this web of interconnectedness becomes even wider. Quite an incredible journey for a common office tool, huh?

As you finish considering and appreciating your stapler, mentally note that you can appreciate all your workplace items (including your clothing!) this way. On your way home from work, try to maintain this perspective—even for a little while—as you note your interrelatedness to all of the other people around you.

"Work" Is a Four-Letter Word—So Is "Play"

What comes to mind when you hear the word "work," as in "I have work to do," "I have to go to work," or "Here's some more work for you"? Does it make you feel joyful and carefree? If so, count yourself as one of the fortunate ones. For the rest of us, "work" has fairly negative or sober connotations. It suggests duty, obligation, seriousness, and a sense of having to do something we don't really want to do. Work also suggests a certain amount of importance or priority. How many times have you excused yourself from some event (such as a party, conversation, or family gathering) because you "had to work"?

Given these associations, it's not surprising that we often have negative feelings about work. We gripe about our jobs, the stress, the workload, and our annoying colleagues. We carry this mindset with us, precluding our ability to experience work differently. Is there any way you can have fun, be silly, or play at work while doing what needs to be done? What a ridiculous question! Yet many innovative companies try to promote this new attitude by making games and fun activities available on site. Google, for example, provides pool, foosball, Ping-Pong, and massage chairs. Employees are allowed to bring their dogs and even to wear their pajamas to work. And these folks work hard, too.

Assuming your company or workplace doesn't have a rock-climbing wall on site or a gourmet cafeteria, how can you have fun there? Here are five ways you can incorporate more play into your workday:

- Notice your attitudes toward work and the tasks you have to do. What judgments pass through your mind? How do you feel? Inspired, resentful, stressed? Curiously examining your thoughts and feelings provides a little emotional distance from them.

- Reorient yourself to the task at hand. What do you need to accomplish? What kind of attitude do you need to do it? Do you need to be serious (perhaps you work in a funeral home), or can you do what's necessary with a smile on your face? See if you can choose what attitude to hold. How does it feel to do so?

- Make a conscious effort to smile more at work. Typically, we embody our emotions. When we feel stressed, we tend to be more stiff, rigid, and unsmiling, for example. Our bodies not only maintain this state but also use it for information on how to feel later, as part of an ongoing feedback loop. We can purposefully change our emotional state by pursuing new activities, considering something in a different light, or adjusting our postures and facial expressions.

Indeed, mimicking the physical embodiment of a particular emotion can lead us to actually experience it. Essentially, we can trick our brains into thinking we feel relaxed even when we're not. For example, it's hard to feel stressed if you're smiling while bouncing up and down, allowing your body to jiggle naturally (literally shaking things up). Don't believe me? Try it for just three minutes. Through this practice, you can recognize some intuitive wisdom in the adage "Fake it till you make it."

- Accept that you don't like certain aspects of your job as you try to identify some positive aspects. Though you might not like your boss, maybe you have lots of autonomy, which you enjoy. Or maybe you don't like making sales calls, but enjoy talking to people. Identify what makes work meaningful for you, and remind yourself of these important values.

- Share a joke or funny story with one of your coworkers. While there are many subjects to *avoid* discussing at work (such as politics, sex, and religion), you can surely find some funny jokes or even "groaners" to tell your colleagues. What? You don't know any jokes? Then try this one: "What did the Zen monk say to the hot-dog vendor? 'Make me one with everything.'"

If you're having trouble giving yourself permission to lighten up at work, it might interest you to learn that taking the time to de-stress can actually improve your efficiency; that is, by allowing yourself to do less, you, somewhat paradoxically, do more! Stress research suggests that we reach a point of maximal efficiency at a medium level of arousal (Yerkes and Dodson 1908). Beyond that point, our performance worsens. Perhaps you can imagine how some athletes psych themselves up for a game and perform really well, while others get too stressed and blow it? This same principle (and underlying physiological mechanism) applies to us and our work, too. So whenever you fear you're about to "choke," give yourself permission to take a fun break, and then check on your work performance afterward. Did you do your job better, worse, or the same? Whatever the outcome, apply what you learned from this experience whenever you find yourself feeling similarly overwhelmed.

Mindfulness First-Aid Kit

Sometimes, we get stuck in a rut and just can't break out. We need a little extra help to disengage from automatic pilot. We might resist sitting in meditation, or find ourselves too distracted when we actually do sit down to meditate. At these times, it can really help to turn to something we previously created or compiled to support mindfulness practice. It might be a collection of songs, a photo album, or a poetry compilation. You can also create a "mindfulness first-aid kit" to use in such situations.

During my clinical internship, I worked with gifted psychologist Lorraine Allman, who used mindfulness in group therapy for people with chronic mental illnesses. As part of the program, she advised participants to develop a "sensory first-aid kit" (Allman 1999, 30), which included items that appealed to each of the person's five senses (that is, sight, smell, hearing, taste, and touch). For example, one participant loved to go to the beach, so she put together a box of things reminiscent of her favorite place, including a postcard (sight), a CD of ocean sounds (hearing), suntan lotion (smell), and saltwater taffy (taste). She then filled the box with sand (touch). When she felt stressed or overwhelmed, she went through her kit and spent several minutes immersing herself in the sensory experience of these objects. Like other people in the group, she not only found herself feeling less stressed, but also really enjoyed taking time out for her mindfulness practice. In fact, she came to see feeling stuck as a positive thing, because it meant it was time to deliberately practice mindfulness! Here are some tips for creating your own mindfulness first-aid kit:

1. Before you even begin, notice your attitude. Do you feel excited, or perhaps pressured to come up with something "creative" or "perfect"?

2. Select a specific place to keep this kit. Do you anticipate needing it most at work, at home, on the bus? You can keep it in a drawer or take it with you in a purse or bag. Determine the most appropriate place to keep it.

3. Select a few items as your go-to objects for mindful attention. Any good first-aid kit includes various medicines and bandages, so your kit should include a variety of objects, too.

4. Don't pick items that will bring up a lot of thoughts. You'll use these things as objects of attention, not inspiration. So, for example, a collection of poems wouldn't be an appropriate selection unless you plan to spend time appreciating the curves of the font instead of considering the content of the passages. Such is the difference between mindful attention and thinking.

As you decide what specifically to include, remember that your items don't need to be related thematically. Simply select objects you find enjoyable. Your kit should be inviting, not off-putting. Here are some more pointers for selecting objects that correspond to each sense:

- Visually, select a picture or object that's not too thought provoking or emotionally stimulating. Something pleasant fits the bill. You don't want to stare at a picture of your ex.

- Tastewise, pick something that has a reasonably long shelf life, like a granola bar or a piece of chocolate. You don't want to store peaches or sushi. Otherwise, you'll find yourself practicing mindfulness of flies!

- For sound, use either a guided meditation or prayer, or a few select songs. Though relaxing and soothing, nature sounds don't lend themselves readily to mindfulness practice. Because these recordings are often looped, they're repetitive, which can lead us to tune things out more easily. Remember, you're looking for something that's easy to use to shake things up.

- For touch, your object can be anything with a notable texture or temperature, like a rock, a piece of fabric, or an instant ice pack. A piece of paper or something similarly smooth might have a texture too subtle to notice easily.

- Because smell is a particularly strong sense for us, many nice possibilities are available. Personally, I really enjoy the aroma of coffee, so I like to keep a few beans handy. You might decide to use an air freshener, a room spray, or even perfume-scented magazine inserts.

- Consider combining some of these sensory elements in a way that makes sense or promotes a peaceful ritual. For example, if you include a tea bag, you can smell it first, feel the warm mug as it brews, and taste it once it's ready.

Pushing Buttons

Regardless of where you work, you push a lot of buttons. If you're an office worker in a high-rise, you push buttons in the elevator and on your computer keyboard. If you work in a café, you push buttons on the cash register, espresso machine, and microwave. If you deliver packages, you push buttons to ring bells and to get signatures on the computerized tablet. You might not even be aware of the degree to which you push buttons all day.

In addition to these physical buttons, we also "push buttons" in our coworkers, colleagues, clients, bosses, patients, and customers. Unlike the deliberate finger poking we do to type a phone number, we're often unaware of the degree to which our actions and speech affect those around us. However, it's simply inevitable that as we relate to people around us, they respond and react, just as we do when they talk to us.

While something we do or say might initially prompt another person's reaction, it has to come through the filter of that person's perceptions, thoughts, emotional states, culture, relationships with others, and entire life history up to that particular moment. That's quite an amazing series of things to consider! Your seemingly benign request for a pen might be directed at a coworker who's having a miserable day and who has never seen his or her loaned-out pens again, which could explain the person's reactive sneer and eye roll. Now, you might be thinking, "So what? It's that person's problem." Indeed, it *is* the other person's problem—but it becomes *your* problem when you're dependent on that person's help to write something down. And it's even more of a problem for you when you allow your own buttons to get pushed by interpreting the other person's response as disrespectful, dismissive, and insulting.

At our jobs, it's generally important to get along well with our coworkers. Typically, we're reliant on their help and support in some way, and it simply feels better to be nice and supportive, as opposed to bitter and vindictive. If treating your colleagues with respect is important to you, please consider some of the following activities:

- Become aware of how you greet and talk to your coworkers. Do you begin with "Hi, how are you?" or immediately start talking about a problem or what you need the other person to do? Do you smile when you talk to others? Essentially, do you give others the same civility and respect you would like to receive?

- As you approach someone, notice that person's behavior, facial expressions, and posture. Do they seem to suggest a particular emotion? If it seems as if the person is having a difficult time, ask one of the most powerful questions: "How can I help?"

- Put particular attention on how your coworkers respond to what you do or say. Notice whether they seem to "react" to something by getting angry or suddenly becoming cold and indifferent. With empathic curiosity, ask what just happened to find out what button you might have pushed.

- Notice when you've made a negative judgment about a coworker. What did this person do or say that led to your assessment? Is it possible that this same circumstance could be interpreted differently? The concept of *fundamental attribution error* in psychology contends that we explain our *own* poor behavior as the result of circumstances while regarding *others'* bad behavior as reflective of their personalities. Given this cognitive bias, is it possible that some external situation could have contributed to the other person's actions?

"What about people who treat me poorly? Do I have to be nice to them?" you ask. In a word, no. But notice the difference in you. How do you feel when you treat an "undeserving" coworker with contempt and disrespect? In contrast, how do you feel when you treat that person compassionately? In all likelihood, the latter situation feels better for you. So, given the choice, doesn't it feel nicer to be nice?

Sensory "Quintathlon"

One of the most demanding physical experiences is to participate in a triathlon. The combination of swimming, biking, and running forces you to use different muscles and transition smoothly between very different, strenuous activities. At work, you can rise to a similar challenge. Presuming you don't have the time (or energy) to suddenly start exercising vigorously, you likely can do a "sensory quintathlon." This event requires you to bring full attention to each of your senses in sequence, which naturally cultivates concentration and awareness in mindfulness practice. The rules for participation are rather simple:

I. Focus your eyes on a particular object or area. Regardless of its distance from you, the object should be about the size of a half-dollar. You might select a spot on the wall or ceiling, for example. Essentially, you want to stay still and keep from moving your head or eyes during this practice.

2. Bring your attention to what you see in this area or object. Notice its color, shape, and shading without resorting to labels (for example, "It's a wall"). As soon as you have an appreciation of how the object or area looks, move on to the next event.

3. Hear what's happening around you. Mindfully bring your attention to everything you can discern. See if you can experience it solely as sound, without labeling the likely source (for example, footsteps, ringing phone, and so on). As soon as you've identified everything you can possibly hear, you're ready for the next stage.

4. Smell your surroundings. By breathing deeply through your nose, see what odors and scents you can detect. Maybe the area smells musty, lemony, or beery? Once you think you've adequately identified the smells in your area, move to the next sense.

5. Tune in to what's happening in your mouth. Notice what tastes might be lingering there from lunch or a recent mint. Does your mouth feel thick and dry, or wet and smooth? What's going on in there? Once you've explored your mouth and tongue, move to the final stage.

6. Notice how your skin feels. Check the temperature of different areas of your body. Your exposed arms in an air-conditioned room might feel cold, relative to covered parts of your torso and legs. Your feet might feel airy or humid, depending on your shoes. Particularly notice where your body makes contact with something. If you're sitting, for example, notice

where the chair touches your legs, buttocks, and back. Once you've thoroughly explored your sense of touch, you're finished!

Congratulations, you have successfully competed in this event. Did you get a fast time? Were you able to cycle through your senses quickly? Oops, I forgot to mention that the winner is actually the person with the slowest time. Better luck tomorrow!

Say, are you interested in a post-event warm down? Within Buddhism, thoughts are considered to be something you perceive, just as are the five senses. If you're up for it, you can end by taking a few moments to check in with your thoughts. Observe what comes to mind. See your thoughts *as* thoughts, rising into and falling from awareness. Spend a few minutes in this space as you prepare to reengage with your work.

Going Up and Down, Mindfully

Oh, the ups and downs of working in the city! Every day, we take stairs and ride elevators and escalators to get from home to work and back. Maybe you don't live in a high-rise apartment or work in a skyscraper but, rather, climb stairs to change trains or get back to your third-floor walk-up. Because all of these up-and-down movements go by relatively quickly on our journey, we tend not to notice them. Yet they can serve as interesting opportunities for mindfulness.

- When riding an elevator or escalator, become aware of your breath. If you're traveling up, pay particular attention to each inhalation. If you're going down, focus on each exhalation. Try not to exaggerate the different aspects of breathing. Remember, the purpose is simply to notice how you're actually breathing.

- Climb and descend stairs slowly, feeling each footfall or bend in your knees. Notice how if feels as your muscles contract to lift your body one step, or how your knees absorb the shock of stepping down. Be aware of any pain, and rest if necessary.

- Practice patience as you wait. The elevator won't move much faster (if at all), no matter how many times you hit the "close door" button. Similarly, escalators move at a preset speed. Allow yourself to be taken for a ride without trying to rush it.

- Use these experiences to transition mindfully between home and work. When you leave one place, imagine leaving all your stress behind. On your arrival at the other place, as you walk through the door, adopt the demeanor you'd like to carry into the space.

- Accept that others need to travel to their destinations too. This means the person walking slowly up the stairs in front of you has as much right to be there as you do. Respect others' personal space; don't tailgate on the stairs or crowd others in the elevator.

Observe what reactions and judgments come to mind as people "violate the rules" of going up and down. Maybe someone stands in the middle of the elevator and makes eye contact. Or maybe someone stands on the "walking" side of the escalator. If you notice yourself making negative judgments, let go of your expectations and see if that feels different to you.

In addition to these practical exercises, consider the process of taking the stairs, elevator, or escalator as a metaphor for how we prioritize different areas of life relative to each other. That is, where you work, live, shop, and see friends might happen at different points from one another in space, with some being physically higher than others. Does this hierarchy of locations reflect your own values? If you live in a basement and work on the 30th floor, does this reflect a priority of your career over your personal life? Of course, any correlations here are simply spurious and coincidental. However, reflecting on these level changes as you move from space to space helps you identify, and take ownership of, the personal significance you place on the different domains of living they represent.

Fern Meditation

Research consistently demonstrates that we feel better when we're connected with nature. A nice, bucolic view from your window has been associated with better recovery from a hospital stay (Ulrich 1984), and having plants in your office has been related to lowered stress and improved productivity (Lohr, Pearson-Mims, and Goodwin 1996). While these studies have not tested other possible stress-relieving distractions (like fish tanks) or alterative explanations (like improved air quality), they suggest that there's something inherently relaxing in viewing nature.

Unfortunately, we spend a lot of time cut off from nature when we live and work in cities. Trees are confined to very small plots on the sidewalk, and you're more likely to see flowers in a florist shop window than growing spontaneously from the ground. If you work in an office, you're surrounded more by plastics and manufactured goods (for example, computers and staplers) than anything occurring organically in nature. However, some workplaces provide a sprinkling of plants as decoration. You can also get a small plant for your work space, even if it's a cubicle, retail store, or taxicab. Many types of plants thrive even with poor lighting and little water. Some hardy indoor plants include the snake plant (*Sansevieria trifasciata*), devil's ivy (*Epipremnum aureum*), Chinese evergreen (*Aglaonema* sp.), and airplants (*Tillandsia*).

To practice this meditation, select a plant to serve as your visual anchor. You'll rest your eyesight and mindful attention on this plant for the duration of the exercise. Ready?

1. Position yourself fairly close to the plant, up to three feet away. Ideally, your field of vision will mainly center on the plant and its pot.

2. Starting from the base of the pot, examine the colors, finish, and presumed texture. Notice the shading on the pot and any reflections on its surface. If you see some dirt, dust, stains, or water droplets, try to perceive them solely through your senses based on their color, shape, and relationship with the rest of the pot. Notice whether your mind passes judgment on these elements—for example, by noting, "It's dirty" or "That's ugly." Bring your attention back to noticing the visual aspects of the pot as you slowly scan its surface toward the top.

3. As your gaze draws upward, spend some time noticing the parts of the plant that might have spilled over the sides of the pot. Maybe you see some leaves or branches hanging over the sides.

4. Select one leaf or branch to notice closely. Invite yourself to notice its shape, color, and shading. Notice that no leaf is merely green. You might notice that some appear olive, gray, brown, or even black. Depending

on the surrounding light, you can detect different shades of color, brightness, reflections, and shadows on any particular leaf.

5. Again, notice any judgments that come to mind. Droopy leaves or brown edges might prompt you to consider watering the plant. A vibrant, healthy plant might lead you to congratulate yourself (or the person who cares for the plants) on a job well done. Whatever evaluations you make, simply note them for later and return to appreciating the visual aspects of the plant.

6. Moving your gaze upward, allow yourself to see more of the plant. Scan the outline of each leaf and branch. Appreciate each fold in the leaves and each tendril of the branch. It might take you a while to examine even a single branch or frond. Notice how your mind wants to move forward or skip over the details of what you see. You might also notice how you lose track of particular leaves and branches as other parts of the plant or pot hide them from view.

7. As you move toward the center of the plant, focus your attention on a spot in the middle while allowing yourself to take in more details with your peripheral vision. Maintain this diffuse visual awareness of the plant for several breaths.

8. Continue your inspection of the plant as you move your gaze upward. Notice how the tips of leaves and branches point skyward. Allow your attention to follow this flow from the plant's tangible surface to open air that's free of form.

9. Nearing the end of the meditation, thank yourself for taking a moment to get grounded during your workday. Also, extend gratitude to the earth for producing such a wonderful, live focus for your meditation. Finally, if necessary, go get that plant a much-deserved drink of water.

Have a Nice Day!

What do you visualize before you start work? Do you imagine yourself managing the day (or night) successfully and calmly? Or do you anticipate all the stressful things that might come up and how overwhelmed you'll feel? Many of us tend to ruminate or "catastrophize" about the negative events we expect to happen at work. Maybe you worry about dealing with irate customers, dread making a phone call, or cringe at the prospect of hurting your back again. Regardless of whether or not these situations are likely to happen, we often don't imagine ourselves handling them well. When we worry, we're prone to focus on how bad something will be, without doing any concrete problem solving or realizing that life will continue even if this anticipated disaster occurs (Leahy 2005).

Before work, rather than worry about the coming day or practice mindfulness during your morning rituals, visualize in a positive way what will happen today. Imagine yourself having a nice day. If you're likely to confront some obstacles or setbacks, visualize managing them well. In fact, research shows that this kind of mental rehearsal improves later performance (Driskell, Copper, and Moran 1994). If you dread making a sales call, for example, you'll likely manage it better if you picture what you'll do and say. The American swimmer Michael Phelps, who set a new record by winning eight gold medals in the 2008 Olympics, uses this mental technique as part of his training regimen. Specifically, he imagines not only each stroke he'll take in the pool but also the ways he'll successfully manage potential setbacks—for example, if his goggles filled with water (Crouse 2009).

Here are the necessary requirements to create the most effective imagery:

- Be as vivid and specific as possible in your visualization. In your mind's eye, picture where you'll be, whom you'll see, how you'll talk, and what you'll do. It's very important to pay attention to detail. The better you can describe or "see" the scene, the more effective it will be.

- You can focus on a very specific situation, like meeting an important deadline, or envision the entire day. As you can tell, creating and envisioning this situation takes time. A review of such rehearsal strategies suggests they should be about twenty minutes long to be effective (Driskell, Copper, and Moran 1994).

- Make a clear distinction between what will happen during the day and how you'll react. Regardless of whether the day's events are positive, negative, neutral, or some combination, imagine yourself managing your work calmly and effectively. If you anticipate having some problems in the coming day, also visualize yourself addressing them productively. This approach is one technique used as part of cognitive therapy for anxiety disorders (Beck, Emery, and Greenberg 1985).

- Envision your day or experience sequentially, from beginning to end. This will help you construct the scene better and recognize all the minute steps that will unfold.

- Smile while doing the visualization, and see yourself smiling within it. When you imagine yourself at work, see yourself smiling and feeling relaxed. As you visualize, try to embody that same sense of peace and calm.

Out and About

Urban Spam Blocker

Living in the city, we are bombarded by ads and written messages whenever we go out. Signs, T-shirt logos, billboards, and flyers litter the visual landscape as we go through our everyday lives. Standing on a street corner in Brooklyn, I was amazed to count twenty-one ads in my line of sight over the course of a minute. Even the relatively simple city garbage truck is festooned with signs, ranging from certification stickers to departmental logos and exhortations like "Don't Litter."

We have spam filters and pop-up ad blockers for our computers, and we go to extensive lengths to ensure safe Internet surfing and to avoid unwanted viruses and e-mails. Unfortunately, nothing like this exists for our urban experience. Written messages and advertising are so intertwined with public settings that we can't remove them. While on a hike in the woods or wading at the beach, you'll see very little (or even zero!) text or ads. But try finding a taxi that doesn't show its name, phone number, and an advertisement; you simply can't do it. Even in our own homes, book spines on the shelf, cereal-box labels, and junk mail exert a subtle influence on our brains and attention. Outdoors, the only alternative is to wear a blindfold (or close your eyes), which I certainly don't recommend, especially when crossing the street.

So we need to find a way to coexist peacefully and mindfully with the city's ubiquity of advertising text and images. In this respect, we have two options: use these messages as a reminder to mindfully focus our attention on some other aspect of our experience, like breathing; or focus more deliberately on the messages, noticing what we see (and what thoughts and feelings arise within us).

- Choose some message or image as a prompt to focus mindfully on something else. For example, perhaps check in with your posture and roll back your shoulders whenever you see an "Open" sign. Or subtly finger your pants seam whenever you see a jeans ad. What you specifically decide to do isn't as important as the process, which prompts you to be more aware and mindfully present in your environment.

- Pay more attention—more mindful attention—to text and images you encounter. When looking at words, simply choose a letter, noting its color and shape. Note your mind's tendency to identify the letter, name the font, or make sense of certain letter combinations. For example, your mind might jump ahead to note that "delivery" is composed of "deli" and "very," instead of simply following the lines and curves of the text. When looking at images, notice what's depicted. What do you see in terms of color, shading, and placement?

As you focus on the ads and signs, be sure to notice what thoughts and emotions arise within you. While noticing an ad for Thai food, you might realize you're hungry, or when you see billboards for luxury goods, you might lament your limited budget. Clothing ads might prompt you to reflect on your own wardrobe or body shape. By encouraging you to be dissatisfied with the way things are, advertising is designed to make you want whatever's being promoted. If you felt content and comfortable with what you have (and don't have) in your life, you'd buy a lot less. So, as you conclude your mindful appreciation of such messages, ask yourself what judgments came to mind and what desires surfaced. By noticing our own reactions in this way, we can become more independent of these influences.

Mindfully Sad in Public

You can't believe this is happening. It's not fair. It doesn't even seem possible, yet it's a heartbreaking reality. How? Why? Words fail to describe the depth of your shock and sadness. As the news slowly sinks in, tears well up in your eyes. So much pain and anguish bubble up from within. You're almost breathless with emotion. Then you realize where you are. "You can't cry here!" screams your brain. Fighting back tears, you struggle valiantly to manage your sadness while considering a more suitable place to cry.

Times of intense sadness like this can be difficult to bear. Of our myriad emotions, sadness seems to be the least acceptable one to display publicly. Opportunities for privacy in the city are few and far between. Unless we're at home alone, we're almost always around other people. And many of us try not to be sad when we think the situation is inappropriate or the place is too public. However, our emotions aren't always so responsive to social norms, circumstances, or our attempts to control them. For example, hearing that a dear friend or relative has died would likely prompt intense grief regardless of where we were. Would we cry? Would we try to control ourselves? How would we express the sudden sadness?

In my experience as a psychologist, I have worked with many people who valiantly tried to suppress painful emotions. They've rejected them, intellectualized them, numbed themselves out (through overeating or drug use, for instance), or avoided situations that prompt them. Usually, the primary reason for such reactions is fear, intense fear over potential catastrophes or fear of the lack of control in letting feelings flow. Akin to holding a big, buoyant beach ball underwater, this process requires you to exert a lot of concentration and strength, and inevitably, you lose control, only to have the ball resurface unexpectedly in a random location. The resultant waves ensure that you—and everyone around you—get splashed with the emotions you were trying to hold down. The healthier, more mindful reaction in such circumstances is to accept what's happening and allow it to surface. In recent years, psychological research has provided evidence supporting this approach, by revealing the negative and counterproductive results associated with suppressing thoughts and emotions (see, for example, Campbell-Sills et al. 2006).

So what does it mean for you to experience a strong emotion like sadness in public? Primarily, you need to accept how you feel and recognize that you can't exactly control your emotions. In fact, controlling them can just be more problematic. In such moments, it's much more helpful to have compassion for yourself in these feeling states. In other words, self-compassion, not self-control, is the answer. Some other practices also facilitate this state of mind.

- Next time you feel a strong emotion, such as sadness, notice your reaction. Do you try to stifle it by keeping your face straight and holding back your tears? Do you look for a corner so you can hide your face when the tears fall? Without judgment, notice what your fears and worries are about, and share the depth of your emotions with those around you, whether they're friends, family members, or strangers.

- Recognize that you're not alone in having emotions. Ask yourself, "Who else might feel like this right now?" In the present moment, there are people all around you in the city who feel sad too. Perhaps this intense experience exemplifies your connection to others.

- Extend kindness and compassion to others when you see them crying or struggling with difficult emotions. Empathize with how they might feel and consider how you feel when you have such emotions. Can you feel a connection to others' emotions even if you don't know why they feel that way?

- Trust that you won't be overwhelmed by how you feel. You might feel intensely sad for a while, but it will pass. Emotions are often compared to waves or weather. In addition to reflecting our inability to control emotions, such comparisons underscore the ephemeral nature of whatever we feel. No matter how intense the emotion, we eventually feel differently. Such is the nature of being human.

Nature, Nature, Everywhere

Despite being surrounded by bricks, steel, and concrete, nature manages to flourish in the city. However, unless we go to a park or community garden, such signs are likely to be subtle—for example, tufts of grass emerging through a sidewalk crack or potted shrubs framing a hotel entrance. Nature isn't limited to plants and vegetation, though. We see squirrels, pigeons, rats, cats, and dogs on a regular basis, too. An observant New Yorker even noted the presence of fish in a puddle in the subway (de Lucia 2008)!

Given the health benefits associated with viewing nature (Park and Mattson 2008), being more aware of plants and animals around us can be helpful. In addition, mindfulness of nature also allows us to notice seasonal changes in the city. Trees, flowers, and plants all grow in accordance with the seasons. For example, vines quickly grow up the sides of buildings during spring and summer, only to die back in fall and winter (assuming you live in more northern cities). Cities with less seasonal variation in weather still experience differences on a daily or weekly basis. For example, a particular constellation of flowers will likely change as blooms die off and get replaced by other ones. Animals, too, are susceptible to these variations. Squirrels that appear plump in summer and fall seem noticeably leaner in spring, after a cold, food-scarce winter. Even dogs get into the act as their owners dress them in sun-shading hats on warm days and sweaters on cold days.

Here are a few suggestions for becoming more mindful of the nature surrounding you:

- Select one patch of greenery you'll notice each day on your commute to work. Pick something relatively small, such as a tree, a window box, or shrubbery. As you pass this area, stop and spend a few moments observing and describing what you see. You might even take a series of digital photos, which allows you to compare how the plants change daily and seasonally.

- Challenge yourself to notice nature around you. Even on the busiest street corner in downtown Singapore, you can see natural objects. You might notice stalks of green bamboo for sale in a Chinatown shop, or see someone deliver a bouquet of roses to an office building, for example. Whatever the circumstances, invite yourself to be on the lookout for nature.

- Nurture a spot of nature close to home or work. Find something growing wild, like a patch of colorful weeds or a city-planted tree, and commit to helping it grow. Perhaps water it weekly, or pick out any accumulated litter. If you'd like to get more involved in this kind of activity, look into municipal resources for trees. Many cities, like New York, Atlanta, and San Francisco, have agencies and organizations dedicated to planting and maintaining trees. Usually, they welcome volunteers to help plant and care for them (like pruning). They also field requests to plant urban trees, in case you'd like to have a nice shade tree in front of your home or apartment building.

- Observe any critters you encounter during the day. On your way to an appointment, maybe stop by your local dog park and spend a few moments watching the dogs run and play with each other. Later, perhaps notice rats moving across the subway tracks (and maybe your corresponding feelings of disgust and revulsion). Even in stores, elevators, and offices, you might be surprised to discover a snout or whiskers poking out from someone's purse or handbag!

Do You Like Live Music?

In 2007, the *Washington Post* (Weingarten 2007) conducted an interesting experiment. It recruited world-renowned violinist Joshua Bell to perform a series of pieces in a busy subway station. Dressed in a T-shirt and jeans while brandishing a Stradivarius, Mr. Bell skillfully played selections by Bach, Brahms, and other great classical composers. Over a thousand people passed within earshot of his forty-five-minute performance, but how many of them stopped to listen?

Consider that here's a *virtuoso* whose performances are always sold out or standing room only. Tickets can cost well over a hundred dollars apiece. He has won the Avery Fisher Prize for "outstanding achievement and excellence in music," and was even selected as one of *People* magazine's "50 Most Beautiful People in the World."

So, did the accomplished artist gather a crowd of aficionados and admirers? No. Out of the thousand or so passersby, only seven stopped for more than a minute to listen to his performance.

In the city, we spend a lot of money on arts and culture. We like to see the latest hit musical, go to plays, attend dance recitals, hear musicians, and laugh at stand-up comics. But we often miss out on these experiences when they arrive in the guise of the street performer.

There are many reasons why we dismiss these experiences. The very fact that the performance is free causes us to devalue it. We're likely to think, *If that guy were any good, he wouldn't be playing here!* Also, we haven't been told what to think of this person's performance yet. No critic or trusted friend has passed judgment, so it's up to us to decide whether we like it. While this invites us to be mindfully present, it also can be intimidating, especially in situations where we're presumed to have an opinion. In addition, we tend to make quick judgments based on our personal tastes. If you already know you don't like classical music, you won't listen to any violinist, stringed quartet, or the like. In some ways, these kinds of judgments are the antithesis of mindfulness. In particular, we don't allow ourselves to hear this music with fresh ears. Maybe, as we expected, we won't like it. However, there's also the possibility that we could be transported to a new emotional place and spark a nascent, avid interest in all things classical. When we hear a street musician, the worst reaction is to resent the intrusion. Such a mind-set not only prevents us from experiencing the music but also makes us miserable with the feeling that something has been imposed on us. (Of course, if you feel this way about a particular street musician, I won't ask you about that dude who practices guitar at the farmers market.) So, rather than pause to appreciate the performance, we turn up the song on our MP3 players and try to drown out the offending music. Contributing to our own hearing loss somehow doesn't seem like the healthiest reaction.

Out and About

1. The next time you pass a street musician (or any street performer), why not pause a moment to observe the spectacle? What notes and sounds do you hear? Does the song seem familiar? If so, see if you can allow yourself to simply hear it as it's played rather then compare it to another performance or jump a few measures ahead.

2. Notice whether you tend to dismiss the performer or the musical genre. What judgments come to mind when you first hear the music or see the performer? See if you can let go of these judgments temporarily and simply listen to the performance. How does it sound? Do you like it or not? If you don't like the music itself, what judgments do you make about the proficiency and enthusiasm of the performer?

3. Finally, notice what comes to mind as you consider donating. Do you feel compelled to give money, or stubbornly refuse to bow to such societal pressure? Do you feel sorry for the musician or guilty if you leave without donating? Notice these thoughts, and return to reflecting on your experience of the performance. If you found some part of it enjoyable, you might consider expressing gratitude to the musician with a simple thank-you, polite applause, a heartfelt "Awesome!" or a modest donation. What was this performance worth to you?

Walking Meditation

Typically, we do a lot of walking in the city—to stores, to restaurants, and to work. In contrast, suburban or rural dwellers spend a lot of time in cars, going from driveway to parking space (and back). Meanwhile, many of us urbanites don't even own cars but rely on walking, biking, public transportation, and taxis.

Walking in the city is not a leisurely stroll. We don't meander down the sidewalk, checking out the architecture or smiling at other people. Instead, we walk purposefully and quickly to our destinations. Often, we tune out en route by listening to music or making calls. Mentally, we distract ourselves, too, by getting lost in our thoughts.

A walking meditation is a powerful way to introduce mindfulness to a very basic human activity. Traditionally, walking meditation is practiced very slowly so we can focus on the physical sensations associated with our bodily movement. However, if we tried to walk that way down a busy street, we'd likely get run over by everyone else. In New York, we have a word for people who walk this way: tourists!

Thus, walking meditations in the city, especially ones you can fold into your daily life, need to be faster. But this requirement is often not conducive to focusing on physical sensations or breathing; we're simply moving too quickly to do so. However, we can change our mental focus to introduce some stress relief as we walk. Specifically, we can adopt a repetitive mental phrase and synchronize it with our steps. Changing our mental focus helps us reduce the aimless distraction associated with rumination, and exercise better control of our attention. Plus, we're practicing a basic form of meditation—albeit quickly—that research associates with stress reduction (see, for example, Benson and Klipper 1976). So here are some guidelines for developing your fast-walking meditation:

1. Decide in advance where and when you intend to start your meditation. I recommend taking at least five minutes for the walk so you can get into the groove.

2. Turn off your electronic devices. You can keep wearing your headphones, but turn off the music. Similarly, you can wear your Bluetooth headset, but turn off the power. You want to be able to hear and see what's around you as you walk.

3. Pick a simple, neutral phrase that you will repeat mentally. When you reach the end of the phrase, repeat it. I suggest picking a phrase relatively benign or descriptive; for example, you could mentally count, *one-two, one-two, one-two,* or say, *I am walking.* You can also experiment with counting your steps from one on; your last number will vary depending on the distance to your destination.

4. Start walking and bringing each successive syllable to mind with each successive step. For example, you might think, *I* (step), *am* (step), *walk-* (step), *-ing* (step), or *one* (step), *two* (step), *one* (step), *two* (step), and so on.

5. Visually, keep looking ahead while remaining aware of your surroundings. You'll likely start to observe the interesting phenomenon that you can concentrate on something artificial (for example, your walking-meditation phrase) while maintaining a responsive awareness of your surroundings.

6. When forced to stop, such as at an intersection or red light, bring your attention to your breathing. Notice the sensations of air entering your nostrils, or the rise and fall of your abdomen and chest. As soon as you can go, resume your walking phrase.

7. When you reach your destination, check in with yourself about your experience of practicing the walking meditation. Did it differ from your usual city walking? If so, how? What will you do similarly or differently next time?

Mindfulness to Go

A unique aspect of urban living is the seeming omnipresence of street vendors selling all kinds of food. No matter where we are, we can always find a quick bite. We don't even have to bother with the laborious task of opening a restaurant door. Pushcarts and trucks abound with all kinds of food options. In fact, you can almost travel the globe, from a culinary perspective. Here are just a few of your options: teriyaki bowl (Japan), pork buns (China), "dirty-water" dog (New York), burrito (Mexico), rice ball (Italy), corn *arepas* (Venezuela), fruit crepe (Belgium), and *halal shawarma* (Middle East). Sounds pretty good, huh?

Such a tremendous variety is very tempting, and the food can be quite delicious. Unfortunately, we don't often take the time to savor its actual taste. The setting and our own activity—standing or walking down the street—make it difficult to pay attention. How can we savor the spicy, salty chewiness of a mustard-laden pretzel while dodging cars in the crosswalk? Also, the inherent messiness of some to-go foods makes us more likely to gulp them down.

So next time you buy some food from a street vendor, take some time to enjoy its flavors. If you've decided to order this particular food and pay money for it, you might as well taste it! Here are some tips:

1. Notice your approach to eating this food. Are you gobbling it down, or can you appreciate its tastes? If you ate it quickly, recall what judgments or perceptions preceded doing so. Were you focused on the experience of eating, or was your mind elsewhere? What thoughts and emotions arise when you consider slowing down?

2. Synchronize your steps with your chewing, by chewing once for each step. This exercise can help you bring more attention to the flavors arising in your mouth.

3. Take one bite every twenty steps, which will help you eat more slowly, also potentially increasing your focus on how the food tastes.

4. Make one bite last a whole block. Keep chewing and tasting a mouthful of food for a whole block before swallowing it. Notice how the urge to swallow and quickly proceed to another bite can arise.

5. Mindfully lick or suck the drippy parts. If your falafel sandwich leaks tahini, mindfully suck the sauce from the bottom, rather than eat faster from the top. Yeah, this might not be the most sanitary activity, but remember, you're the one who chose to eat in the middle of the street.

6. Sit down to eat for a while. Just because you bought some on-the-go food doesn't mean you need to keep going! Take several minutes to sit and enjoy your food. You might also notice what you see in the city scene before you.

7. Practice mindfulness of eating (you'll need to stop walking to do this one). Prior to each bite, smell your food's aroma. What can you detect? Any particular spices? As you bite down, notice how your mouth greets the food. Do you detect an increase in your salivation, or does your tongue curl up? As you slowly chew, move the food around in your mouth. See how you detect more distinct flavors of saltiness, bitterness, sourness, and sweetness, depending on where the food is on your tongue. Notice the urge to swallow before you actually do. What's transpiring in this moment? Are you poised to take another bite before you've even finished and swallowed this one? After each bite, see how long you can detect that mouthful of food in your body. Can you feel it go down your throat? Can you feel it in your belly? Do you feel as if you're one mouthful heavier?

Awareness of the Homeless

In the city, we see the homeless almost every day. Verbally or with written signs, they tell us a sad story and seek donations for food, shelter, or transportation. They're often willing to take "even a penny" to get a little closer to their goals. We typically respond by looking away, developing a sudden interest in our books or phones, or digging into our pockets to produce some spare change. All of these efforts are designed to minimize our discomfort with the situation by allowing us to move on as fast as possible. Seeing someone suffer close up can be simply too much to bear.

Homeless people also bring up many automatic judgments. Some of us feel sorry for the person. Some of us assume the person is a drug abuser or criminal. Others assume the person's crazy or unstable. Some blame homeless people for their circumstances and shout, "Get a job!" Others blame society, and consider the homeless to be victims of our misplaced priorities and resources. Depending on the reaction, we likely feel sympathetic, hardened, guilty, generous, or scared. However, in the moment, all these assessments are wrong; they're based on preconceptions rather than actual engagement with the homeless person.

I'm not suggesting you run out and start talking to every homeless person you meet. There are many valid reasons why you might decide not to do that. However, that moment of encounter can be a very powerful lesson in mindfulness. Can you become aware of your thoughts about the person without getting carried away by them? Can you simply be, even in the presence of something or someone very challenging? Is there a way to enter into the experience of being with or seeing a homeless person without prejudging it? The original mindfulness sutra in Buddhism contains instructions on how to meditate while watching dead bodies decay. The purpose is to deal with discomfort and appreciate the ephemeral nature of life. Observing a homeless person can deliver similar messages to us.

Indeed, there are many spiritual traditions that espouse compassion and support for others. The Bible is filled with references to "love thy neighbor." Buddhism encourages the practice of loving-kindness toward others. Judaism speaks of such duties as helping others through charity (*tzedakah*) and living in accordance with religious commandments (*mitzvot*). Out of respect for the wisdom of these traditions, as well as our own desire to be more mindful, are we willing to practice mindfulness even in respect to the homeless? Here are some ways to approach these situations:

- Extend a blessing of protection and wellness to the homeless person. Mentally send a quiet wish that this person find a way to be happy, healthy, and whole.

- For as long as you're in the presence of the homeless person, see if you can breathe in the person's suffering, while breathing out compassion and kindness. This *tonglen* practice from Tibetan Buddhism addresses our tendency to push away painful experiences. You might also imagine taking in the heaviness or darkness of the person's difficulties, while sending out lightness and brightness.

- If the person asks for money or something else, can you be mindful of your decision whether or not to give? How does your judgmental mind react to your decision? Do you feel like a helper, a sucker, an uncaring lout? Whatever your response, notice what comes to mind about yourself and the homeless person.

- Consider how you might feel if your circumstances were reversed: What if you were the person without a home, money, or other resources? How would it feel for you to beg for money? How would you want passersby to treat you?

- If the situation seems safe, see if you have the courage to talk with the homeless person directly. Ask about the person's circumstances and the reason behind any requests made of you. What judgments come to mind as you interact with this person? Does the story seem compelling, plausible, or unbelievable? What does this person want or need? Given your resources and judgments of this person, what are you willing to do?

Subway Meditation

As urbanites, we typically spend a lot of time using public transportation. Subways, buses, trains, and trolley cars all serve to take us to our destinations. More often than not, we spend this time immersed in distractions en route. We read books, listen to music, play video games, and catch up on e-mails and text messages. Rather than tune out, however, we can use this time to practice meditation.

While it's not ideal in terms of providing a quiet, relaxed atmosphere, we can indeed try to meditate while using public transportation. The key to meditating in this way is to turn our attention to what's happening in our bodies. We can bring our attention to our breathing or our thoughts, but typically, I advise people to become aware of their somatic sensations as they move along. For example, if you're standing on the subway, you're likely to experience sensations in your feet from the car's rumbling, and tensing of various muscle groups as you try to maintain balance. Bringing your attention to this experience helps you eventually integrate a mindfulness practice into your daily commute.

Before I provide some guidelines for this kind of meditation, let me issue a word of caution: Always be aware of your safety and the environment around you. Particularly in urban areas, which are more prone to violence and crime, we must be vigilant to ensure our own protection. So when it comes to meditating on the subway, be sure it's a risk-free place to do so. If you see anyone who looks suspicious, menacing, or erratic, it's probably best not to meditate but, rather, to maintain your focus on your personal safety.

Though there are different ways to meditate on public transportation, depending on whether you stand up or sit down, some commonalities exist between the two situations:

1. Be sure to meditate with open eyes. Gently rest your gaze on something in front of you. Perhaps look at a spot on the floor or wall, rather than at a specific person. Otherwise, you risk getting interrupted by a brusque "What are *you* looking at?"

2. Turn off your MP3 player, but consider keeping the earphones on to reduce the likelihood that someone will disturb you.

3. Focus your attention on your body's physical sensations. Either maintain awareness of one area of your body (like your feet), or systematically scan your body, starting from your feet and working your way up to your head.

4. Whenever the train stops, take a moment to check whether this is your stop. Although it disrupts the flow of your meditation, each stop serves as a gentle

reminder to return your attention to your body; it helps you catch your mind's occasional drifting.

For a standing meditation, it's important to maintain your balance, so it's best to stand with your feet about shoulder-width apart. Try to position your feet at a forty-five-degree angle from the train's centerline, if possible. Roll your shoulders back, and raise your chin up to keep your head level. Mentally focus on whatever bodily feelings are prompted by the movements of the train or bus. In particular, notice the way your feet and leg muscles tense and release to help you maintain balance. You might also become aware of a shift in your body weight as the car accelerates and brakes.

For a sitting meditation, try bringing your attention to your breathing or your body. If you focus on your breathing, simply notice the gentle rhythm as you inhale and exhale. You can choose to notice the sensation of air entering and exiting your nostrils, or the rise and fall of your chest and abdomen. If the subway is particularly smelly, try focusing on breathing through a slightly open mouth, making sure to keep your jaw relaxed. If you focus on your body, simply notice the bumps that happen as you move along and the tightening of different muscle groups as you react to the car's movement.

Spend as much time as you'd like in this activity, depending on your commute time. Once you've reached your destination, exit carefully and congratulate yourself on taking a few moments to introduce mindfulness to your day.

Zen Mind, Tourist Mind

You've seen them on the street. They walk slowly, gawk openly, talk loudly, and wear fanny packs unabashedly. I'm talking, of course, about the bane of urban existence: tourists. Unfamiliar with the surroundings, tourists spend considerable time taking in the city's details. Of course, they get in our way, and have the audacity to smile and make eye contact on the subway. Such flagrant disregard for the rules of city living earns them scorn, yet they're probably more aware of what's happening than we locals are!

As we go about our daily lives, we soon develop a routine based on our typical work schedule, commute, weekly chores, and preferred activities. We take the same subway train, go to the same workplace, see the same coworkers, and go to the same grocery. And we go to the same parks, theaters, bars, and clubs. As our lives become more predictable, practicing mindfulness becomes more difficult. We become habituated to our surroundings and pay less attention to them. Research demonstrates that we tend to better appreciate novelty than familiar things (Chong et al. 2008).

The particular bus we take today looks almost exactly like the one we took yesterday, so it receives little additional attention or consideration.

In particular, we tend to tune out while on the way to another of our predictable destinations. Sometimes we're lost in thought, lingering on something that happened before we left home or on what we expect to greet us once we arrive at our destination. At other times, we purposefully try to distract ourselves by reading, listening to music, or typing text messages. Alternatively, we might be embroiled in lively conversation with a friend, partner, or fellow passenger. In all of these circumstances, we don't notice what's happening around us as we travel.

Maybe it's time to act like a newcomer in your own city. I'm not suggesting that you check out all the local tourist traps (be careful of your judgments here) but, rather, that you start seeing and experiencing your life in the city as if for the first time. Here are some suggestions for invoking such a fresh perspective:

- Carry a camera and take pictures of the area around your home and workplace. By taking a few photos (or even one) every day, you start to look at the world in a different way. Visually examine your surroundings for interesting and photogenic things. You'll start to notice shapes, patterns, and the interplay of light throughout the day, all of which are essential elements of photography that help you develop awareness of your environment.

- Look up. Many of the buildings around you have interesting architectural details, which you'll miss if you only look ahead or keep checking your e-mail. See if you start to recognize similarities in architectural styles as you travel around the city.

- Notice what tourists get excited about. Maybe you spot some people who are entranced by a particular monument or other attraction. What judgments do you make about what they like or find interesting? Are you dismissive and critical? Have you actually experienced what they find fascinating? Try to take a step back from your cynicism and note what's interesting or engaging about this attraction.

- Smile. People usually have a good time when they travel, so they're apt to smile and laugh. Adopt a smile yourself, perhaps allowing your city's tourists to prompt you.

- Offer to help a visitor if the person seems lost or needs some guidance. Through your kind assistance, you'll not only serve as a goodwill ambassador on behalf of your city, but also possibly feel happy afterward.

- Practice acceptance of, and patience toward, tourists struggling with being in an unfamiliar place or violating the city's unwritten rules. You might get stuck behind someone who's trying to figure out how to use an automated ticket dispenser or ATM. Or someone might do something that's verboten in your neighborhood, like spitting in the street or walking on the wrong side of the sidewalk. Whatever the affront, bring awareness to your annoyance. If necessary, discreetly offer some advice if you think the offense is serious enough to warrant correction.

Out and About

Through these and other relatively simple practices, we can become mindfully aware of the city again, plus we start noticing our critical judgments. It all takes practice to ensure staying on track. Of course, if we really want to embody a tourist's perspective, the most effective way is obvious: take a trip!

Window to the Inside World

One of the fundamental properties of mindfulness is the ability to notice what's happening in the present as it unfolds moment to moment. Life and our surroundings are constantly changing and in flux; for example, the breeze on your skin changes as you walk down the street. The dynamic nature of our experience can be even subtler. What you're thinking, feeling, and doing right now—at the beginning of this sentence—even differs from what you're thinking, feeling, and doing right now—at the end of this sentence. Your eyes are now focused on a different part of this page, for example. Change also occurs beyond the detection of our normal sensory experience. Scientists note that our bodies constantly change on an atomic and molecular level as well; for example, old cells die and are replaced by new ones in our skin, internal organs, and brain (see, for example, Eriksson et al. 1998).

Meditation provides a way for us to become aware of change by focusing on our bodies' shifting conditions. We notice our discursive thoughts, tingling legs, and periodic bouts of itchiness (if not the growth of neurons in the prefrontal cortex). With practice, we can appreciate how meditation provides an observation point for these internal fluctuations. Over the years, I have used various metaphors to describe this observational process, such as stepping out from under the waterfall of thoughts that cascades and inundates the mind, or standing on a platform watching the trains of thought pass by. While these examples provide an interesting perspective on the process, you can also take them somewhat literally, thus providing a sensory way to appreciate the ephemeral, dynamic nature of your surroundings. Now, I'm not suggesting running out and getting underneath a waterfall, but you can stand still and observe, becoming aware of the changing information you receive from your senses. If you're in a crowded café, you can attend to the various sounds you perceive, such as music, conversation, bursts of steam, clanking plates, and so on. On the street corner, you can pause and see what enters and exits your field of vision, perhaps including pedestrians, cars, and passing clouds.

A more concrete example in which we can notice change while remaining slightly removed from the experience is looking out the window. When we do so, we can view the unfolding scene before us without directly participating in the experience. If you'd like to try this exercise, here are a few pointers:

1. Select a spot where you can look out a window for a few minutes. It can be a window in a restaurant, store, or even a bus.

2. Focus your attention on what's happening outside the window.

3. Pick a specific point or object of reference and then draw your attention back several feet toward you. Don't concentrate on the object at that point, but rather try

to detect movement within your visual field. Things might look, or even feel, a little spacey to you in this diffuse state of awareness.

4. Notice what movement and variations you detect. See how things come and go, stop and start. You might, for example, notice people passing in and out of your field of vision, or leaves blowing in the wind. Even things that emerge in your awareness very powerfully—like a fast car or strong gust of wind—soon disappear.

5. Spend a few minutes in this practice, simply breathing and watching. Let your face and jaw muscles soften.

6. As you close this practice, consider what you observed. How does this process compare to experiences within you?

Anytime, Anywhere

Patience Is a—
Hey, Where's My Bus?

In life, we spend a lot of time just waiting. In the morning, we might wait for our toast to cook or tea to brew. In the afternoon, we might wait for some photocopies to print. In the evening, we might wait for a bus or taxi. Sometimes the wait can be longer than the duration of the event we're waiting to participate in. For example, it might take fifteen minutes of standing in line at the store in order to complete a speedy checkout. Often, we get impatient. We try to distract ourselves while waiting, or anxiously ruminate about why it takes so long, but in doing so, we essentially reject whatever's happening in the present moment. We become less aware of our surroundings, make more judgments about the unacceptability of what's happening, and strive to have something else, other than what is. We react negatively to the fact that things aren't as we want them to be. And, indeed, we're correct: the toast isn't fully cooked, the copier isn't finished printing, and the bus is nowhere to be seen.

Waiting, of course, can happen anytime, anywhere, and for any duration. To a certain degree, it's relative. You might be waiting for your daughter to hurry up and go to college even though she just started high school. Or you might feel anxious while waiting for your food to arrive, because you feel starved. The essential issue is how we approach these waiting periods, in terms of both our actions and our attitudes.

Typically, when we're waiting, we find ways to distract ourselves by reading a book, checking e-mail, or listening to music, instead of simply allowing ourselves to be. Indeed, waiting rooms usually provide some entertainment for distraction, like magazines or a TV, presumably to take our minds off the fact that the office is behind schedule. Sometimes we might use these moments as opportunities for meditation or mindfulness practice. But usually we just tune out. Distraction isn't necessarily bad. In fact, it can be a very effective strategy for enduring pain or distress (Kleiber and Harper 1999). The distinction lies mainly in your underlying attitude toward what's happening in the present. Do you resent the wait and feel desperate to move on, making yourself miserable as you try to focus on your book? Or do you wholeheartedly accept your present experience of waiting, while turning your attention to an interesting novel?

Given that waiting is a reality of our existence, we have little choice but to find a way to be in these moments. When things are poised to be the way we want them, but they're not quite there, what kind of attitude is healthiest or most effective? In the present, is it best to keep focusing on something we expect or want to have in the future, or, similarly, to ruminate on what happened in the past?

For much of life, things happen when they happen. The bus arrives when it arrives, not necessarily when it *should* arrive. Our soup is warm when it's warm, as a function of how much heat it receives over time. We can generally do things to influence this process, like take a different bus route (or write a complaint letter to the transit authority) or buy a more powerful microwave, but even in those moments, we're still waiting—waiting while wishing for some other experience.

- Notice how your body responds to waiting. Do you keep looking down the street for the bus? Do you keep hitting the elevator's "close door" button? Whenever the urge to reject your waiting time surfaces, see if you can bring your attention to the moment before taking action. Resist the urge, and instead bring your attention to the experience of *not* acting on it. How does this feel?

- When waiting, bring your attention to your breathing. Notice each breath going in and out of your body. Consider this time as a precious opportunity to practice mindfulness and integrate awareness into your daily life.

- Notice your facial expression. What kind of face are you making? Are you carrying any stress or tension in your brow or jaw? See if you can change your relationship to this present moment of waiting by greeting it openly and with a slight smile.

Hey, That's Mine!

We urbanites can easily develop a competitive streak while striving to meet our daily needs. We tend to suspect that others are threatening to take away something we desire, like that subway seat or that parking spot across the street. In some areas, people lay claim to the parking spots in front of their homes by blocking them with garbage cans. You take the spot at the risk of having your car vandalized or, at the very least, incurring the wrath of the home owners.

Perhaps the crowdedness of urban life or an accumulation of experiences where someone else beat us to our rightful place in line prompts us to become very possessive and defensive of things and experiences that really don't belong to us at all. Recently, in a store someone exclaimed to me, "Hey, that's mine!" when I selected a broccoli stalk to put into my cart. Though she was all the way on the other side of the aisle, she believed she had rights to it because her eyes presumably fell on it before my hand did.

Biologists and economists argue that such competitiveness often emerges out of our desire for scarce resources (see, for example, Moore 1999). Not surprisingly, we also tend to evaluate scarce resources as being better than the same things when abundant (Mittone and Savadori 2009). This is consistent with the basics of supply and demand: a limited supply combined with a high demand means you can set a higher price. In other words, a parking spot in front of your favorite city art museum is much more valuable than one at the suburban mall.

What does this kind of possessiveness or competitiveness get us? Sure, we might succeed in getting something we want, but this state of mind also prompts us to feel stressed and defensive—plus, it can easily lead to anger and conflict (Griskevicius et al. 2009). I've seen many arguments erupt over taxicabs, for example. When a taxi pulls over, whose is it? Does it belong to the person who saw it first, whoever's closest, or the one who has been waiting the longest time? The correct answer, of course, is always, "It's mine!"

Mindfulness can be a helpful touchstone to realistically assess our judgments and curb excessive emotional reactions. By becoming aware of your own perspective on why you believe something is yours, you can see implicit assumptions that might not even be accurate. For example, the broccoli lady in the store became quite embarrassed when I offered to give her the desired vegetable, especially when we both recognized that the bin was full of other stalks. Even when our assessment is correct—maybe there *is* only one stalk left—mindfulness can help us be less angry and potentially work out a satisfying solution. The woman could have bargained with me for the broccoli or considered other vegetables after I took it. By gaining some distance from her emotional reaction, she would at least *feel* better, even if she wound up making cauliflower for dinner instead.

So the next time you tell yourself (or someone else) that something in a public space rightfully belongs to you, here are a few tips:

1. Bring your attention to the emotions, such as anger, stress, or fear, that arise in your body.

2. Ask yourself, "What makes this mine?" or "Whom does this belong to?"

3. Talk with your competition about your shared difficulty (that is, you both want the same thing at the same time). Perhaps you can both take advantage of the situation (for example, sharing a cab), or maybe together you can determine which of you should take it (for example, letting the person who's late for a meeting have the cab). While you might not get what you want or "deserve" when negotiating a solution, the process can greatly decrease your stress, especially when you might not have gotten the object of your desire anyway.

4. Give whatever it is away to your competitor freely and with your blessings. Here, you're making the choice to forego something in exchange for peace of mind and less stress. You'll have to deal with going without whatever you gave up, but at least you can feel better about your act of kindness.

Congestion, Frustration, and Aggravation

Living and working in the city means spending a lot of time in crowds and stuck in traffic. You might be packed into a bus or stuck in your car, immobilized by rush-hour traffic. You also get surrounded by throngs of people as you exit a theater, sporting event, or subway station. In such situations, you can be literally face to face, elbow to elbow, back to back, and even belly to belly with a bunch of strangers. And you get frustrated.

Research shows that being in crowded environments is inherently stressful. Put too many rats in a cage and they get sick (Dronjak et al. 2004). Put too many monkeys in a cage, and they start to fight (Boyce et al. 1998). Not surprisingly, your human stress response also gets activated when you're in a crowded place. The release of stress hormones reflects the well-known fight, flight, or freeze response's activation. As you're probably aware, in stressful situations like these, your body prepares to run away, fight someone, or stay completely immobile. A host of physiological changes facilitates these hardwired responses: your heart and respiration rates increase to better distribute oxygenated blood throughout your body; you start to sweat, which cools your body and makes it more slippery (and thus less likely to be grabbed by a predator); and blood rushes to major muscle groups to facilitate action. Though they help you survive a life-threatening situation, these wonderfully adaptive responses aren't so helpful when you're standing in a crowded subway car. You can't pry open the doors and run for safety, and you (hopefully) don't start picking a fight with the person next to you. What *do* you do? In a word, nothing. Is there a way to change the situation? No. You're stuck, and there's no place to go. It will be stressful. But you don't have to add to the stress by piling on a host of judgmental thoughts and attitudes.

Typically in situations like these, you'll reflect on what's happening around you, and you won't likely think too positively. All kinds of unproductive thoughts will flood your mind, making this bad situation even worse: *It's too hot, Get out of my way! Did you just push me? It shouldn't be this crowded,* and *I can't take this anymore!* Unfortunately, all of these thoughts add suffering to an already unpleasant situation.

"So, how can mindfulness help?" you ask. "Why would I even want to become more aware of how miserable this situation is?" You don't. However, mindfulness is about more than just awareness. It's also about acceptance, curiosity, and nonjudgment. Here are several ways to experience this bad situation differently, even though you can't do anything about it:

1. Notice what's passing through your mind. What do you tell yourself about the situation? What do you think about yourself, about the people around you?

Does having these thoughts help you feel better or worse?

2. Notice whether you're dragging the past or future into the present. Do any of your thoughts relate to things that aren't happening now? Do you tell yourself you'll be late, for example? Maybe you recall a prior time when you had a panic attack in similar circumstances. In either case, your dreaded situation isn't happening yet, is it?

3. Now ask yourself whether you're willing to practice accepting the present moment. You feel distressed and don't want to be in this situation. What happens if you give up your desire for things to be different than they are now? What happens if you surrender yourself to the present moment?

4. Invite yourself to consider your experience relative to the people around you. Are they having a better time than you are? Most likely, you're all suffering together. Sometimes it's comforting to know you're not alone.

5. Finally, introduce a new perspective relative to the people around you. See if you can identify some-thing—besides the present moment—that you might have in common with them.

Hurry Up and Slow Down

City life is fast and dynamic. Things and people move quickly. Taxis and bike messengers career down the street, people walk briskly, and police officers give you a parking ticket (and disappear) within the two minutes it takes for you to run into the bagel shop for change. City life is fast, indeed!

Because we live and work in this high-paced environment, we start to go faster too. We talk fast, move fast, drive fast, and think fast. Unfortunately, our higher speed can have negative consequences. Consistent with the adage "Haste makes waste," research shows that increased speed and time pressure cause us to make more mistakes (see, for example, Wickelgren 1977). Yet despite this obvious disadvantage, we continue to rush.

Our expectations eventually come to match this hurried lifestyle. We want our Chinese food delivered before we hang up the phone. In conversation, we want the other person to get to the point quickly. And on city sidewalks, we expect others to walk just as quickly as we do or get out of the freakin' way!

When things and people don't move as fast as we want or expect, we get frustrated and annoyed. Sometimes our annoyance can flow easily into righteous indignation: "What do you mean I have to wait for coffee to brew? You're a coffee shop! You should have coffee ready all the time!"

More often than not, life doesn't move as fast as we want. We inevitably have to wait for things we'd prefer to have instantly. At a restaurant, for example, the waiter doesn't immediately make our meal materialize on order; it takes time to prepare, even if we're really, really hungry.

When you feel pressured to move quickly or have something immediately, take some time to do the exact opposite: slow down.

- Stay still and take a few deep breaths. In making this effort, you might notice your body reflecting how antsy or frustrated you feel by bouncing up and down, pacing, or not breathing deeply. Observe the thoughts that come to mind. Are they familiar? Do they reject the apparent slowness of what's transpiring in the present?

- Explore ways to appreciate things that move slowly or take time. Buy a cactus and watch it grow. Make a meal from scratch. Race turtles.

- Ask yourself, *Is there anything I can do to speed up this process?* If the answer is no, practice acceptance.

- Investigate Slow Food (www.slowfood.com), a worldwide organization with over a hundred thousand members, that's dedicated to helping people appreciate the benefits of living slowly by eating fresh, local, seasonal foods.

- Check to see if there's a slow *movement* group in your city. Similar to the one previously mentioned, these groups also advocate slowness in other areas of life, like commuting and socializing. London has a growing slow movement community where people commit to "living life in real time" (slowdownlondon.co.uk). Maybe you can join a local group or create such an organization in your own city.

Lonely Is As Lonely Does

If you've ever driven in the country or hiked in the woods, you've undoubtedly had the thought *There's no one around for miles!* In these places, often we can go for vast stretches of time and distance without seeing signs of others. Not so in the city! People are all around us. In fact, we literally live and work on top of each other in high-rise apartments and office buildings.

Despite being around people so much, we often complain of loneliness. We feel alone despite a seemingly endless stream of opportunities to connect with those around us. Usually, people don't come up to us to talk, nor do we talk to them. This circumstance will likely get worse as we increasingly use advanced communication devices that actually keep us isolated by screening our calls or leaving us "invisible" to online friends (Baron 2008).

Let's do a little thought experiment. Suppose I ask you to consider talking to the person beside you the next time you're in line. What reactions do you have? What thoughts come to mind? You might wonder what to say or how the person might react to you.

You think, *That's just too weird!* Emotionally, you might find yourself feeling excited about, scared of, intimidated by, nervous about, or dismissive of this idea. Notice your reaction in the present moment as you consider doing something outside your usual comfort zone.

Sometimes people wonder, *What would I even say?* In such circumstances, mindfulness can really help, because it provides an opportunity to discuss what's happening in your shared experience of the present moment. Of course, you (and the other person) need to attend to what's happening to discuss it. After offering a smile and a simple hello, you can readily ask a question or reflect on what's happening:

- "Man, this line is really slow, huh?"

- "What movie are you going to see?"

- "This is my first time in this deli. Have you been here before? What do you recommend?"

- "That's a nice shirt."

- "It feels so cold today."

In reaching out, you need to realize that you can't control how the person responds. The person might be friendly and engaging, or rude and dismissive. You won't know until you try to connect. The potential reward in having a nice conversation or making a new friend necessarily involves the risk of rejection. If you don't try, you're pretty much guaranteed to continue feeling lonely. Before you attempt conversation, you feel alone. In the worst-case scenario of talking to a stranger, the person rebuffs you and you still feel lonely. The best-case scenario is that you find the love of your life or make a new friend. Isn't that worth the risk?

Mindful Messaging

In the twentieth century, people often communicated by writing letters, typically by hand. It took time and effort to compose your thoughts and convey them in an effective, considerate way. Etiquette and formatting rules soon developed to improve communication. For example, in her original 1922 etiquette guide, Emily Post noted that correspondence to friends, family, and romantic partners should always be handwritten. Letter writing was a deliberate exercise, because you carefully chose words to communicate well, avoid offense, and preserve ink and paper. The whole process was time consuming, because it included not only writing the letter but also addressing the envelope and physically mailing it.

Today, this process seems grossly inefficient or antiquated, or quaint at best. Over the past several years, the availability and speed of communication has grown exponentially. Technology allows us to communicate with each other more easily and quickly. Interestingly, many of these technologies don't involve our actually talking with another person but, rather, sending short updates in text messages or on social-networking sites like Facebook, MySpace, and Twitter. By not talking to the other person—either in person or over the phone—we lose the ability to discern subtle messages and emotional meaning. Imagine meeting a friend for a rushed meal before dashing away to a doctor's appointment. Later, you receive the text message "Gr8 2 C U." Is this a heartfelt expression of appreciation or a passive-aggressive criticism? It's hard to tell based simply on the text. Interestingly, using emoticons and punctuation as facial expressions seems to have developed in response to this lack of emotional clarity.

Whether it's the lack of face-to-face contact, the ambiguity of the messages we receive, or the immediate accessibility of communication, we tend to react much more emotionally through our text or e-mail messages, which creates problems, especially if the recipient feels (justifiably) attacked. The person becomes defensive and critical in response to our messages. As a result, a simple inconvenience, annoyance, or misunderstanding quickly escalates into a full-fledged fight, threatening our commitment to a friend or partner. At work, it can prevent us from collaborating constructively with someone. At the very least, texting in anger or under stress usually causes more problems than it resolves.

Many of us also send text or e-mail messages on the go, which recently has been associated with an increase in accidents, as drivers become more engrossed with their phones than what's happening on the road. Even pedestrians face this obstacle: it's impossible to see where you're going when your head is down and your attention is consumed by reading and writing text messages.

Clearly, given these considerations, we need to bring more awareness to how we communicate with these new technologies. These suggestions cover a variety of circumstances:

- When you receive a text message, especially one that prompts anger or sadness, take a few moments to breathe. You can respond later, but first breathe and allow yourself to settle into your body. Notice what judgments your mind makes about this particular message. Invite yourself to consider other possible ways to interpret this message. Would a stranger also feel attacked or criticized by it?

- After you write a message, especially one relative to something that prompted you to feel angry or stressed, take a few deep breaths. Read your message and imagine how you would feel if you received it. Would you feel happy, angry, attacked, dismissed? Do you want the recipient to feel this way? If not, rewrite the message to reflect the emotional tone you want to convey.

- Remember the past and consider the future in the present. Some of our missives are readily available to *all* of the people around us, especially the updates we post on social networking websites and blogs. So, in the present moment, as you're poised to gripe about work on your home page, it's helpful to recall that your boss has the URL. Also, it's well known that the Internet has a long memory or "tail." People can see the info you post now for years to come. In fact, many employers regularly conduct Internet searches on the names of job candidates to learn more about them. With this in mind, do you feel comfortable with the idea that future friends, partners, and employers can possibly view what you're writing?

- Stay still when you're messaging. Is it really so time consuming to sit down for a moment to write a text message or send an e-mail? Although this is based loosely on a Zen Buddhist directive, think of it this way: Walk when you're walking. Text when you're texting. Above all, don't walk and text!

- Extend love, kindness, and support to people in your network. Sometimes we can use texting or micro-blogging to focus too much on our own experience. Is it really so important for all of your friends to know what you're eating for lunch? If these relationships are important to you, perhaps an encouraging note or inspiring message would be more appropriate. Recognize what you're actually communicating over time, and the degree to which it reflects ego-driven messages rather than compassion for those who matter in your life.

Mindfulness Emergency!

Urban living can be very loud. Traffic, nightclubs, and construction all contribute to quite a noisy landscape. In fact, noise pollution has gained recognition as a significant problem over the past few decades. Research indicates that noise is the leading cause of people's dissatisfaction with their neighborhoods and one of the principal reasons people move (U.S. Environmental Protection Agency 1981). In recognition of this problem, some cities, like Paris and San Francisco, have even developed noise "maps" outlining the average decibel levels in different areas at different times of day.

Ambulance, fire engine, and police car sirens are one of the noisiest and most disconcerting city sounds. At about 120 decibels, sirens are about as loud as a jet engine during takeoff. Typically, when we hear a siren, we do one of four things: cover our ears; turn up the TV, stereo, or MP3 player volume; talk louder; or wince stoically while waiting for it pass. Three of these actions actually contribute to worse hearing loss and constitute rejection of the present moment. Can you tell which ones? The healthy, mindful action is to simply cover our ears. Reflecting awareness of our pain, it's an appropriate action relative to a situation we must accept (that is, we can't turn off the siren). Some people might think the stoic response reflects mindfulness and acceptance. While it engenders recognition of the noise and suggests a pause in our ongoing activity, it also rejects a very natural, normal response (covering our ears). Often, we employ judgments or forecasting, by considering this action to be "wimpy" or anticipating that the noise won't last long. Neither of these attitudes accepts the painful reality ringing in your ears, which leads you to take the protective action—presuming, of course, that in covering your ears, you do so lightly and without malice. No cursing the siren or telling yourself you can't stand it!

Besides preserving our hearing by covering our ears, we can use siren sounds to suggest a mindfulness emergency. Most likely, we've been engaged in doing something while tuned out from our surroundings. Or we're about to act in a very unmindful way. So, the siren can act as a wake-up call to practice mindfulness. Here are a few strategies to use:

- As soon as you hear the siren, focus on your breathing. Notice each in-breath and out-breath throughout the siren's duration. Keep returning your awareness to your breath, as if it were a true emergency.

- Send compassionate or loving wishes to the rescuers and whoever's in need. The siren signifies that someone's in trouble. Rather than damning the interruption, why not extend some kindness toward whoever needs help? Extend a wish that all the people involved get through the ordeal safely and in good health.

- Mindfully notice the siren's variations in pitch and loudness. Stay aware of the siren's initial sound as it progressively fades away. Meditation halls typically use a bell or cymbal to reorient people to the present moment, while inviting them to attend to the sound. We can use sirens similarly, even if they aren't as soothing or pleasant.

- Notice your own reactions to and judgments about the siren. Do you react with anger at the loud noise? Are you nervous and stressed while waiting for it to pass? Do you damn this disruption of your life, as the offending car or truck slows traffic flow? Whatever thoughts and feelings arise, simply note them as reactions to your unpleasant experience in the present moment.

All of these strategies can help us experience our noisy environment a little differently. Instead of rejecting loud disturbances, we can see them as an opportunity to practice mindfulness. We all need such reminders from time to time, and perhaps we can even be thankful for them. It sure beats what we usually do, no?

Mindfulness of Diversity

The relatively high populations of urban areas provide ample opportunities for encountering ethnic diversity. Indeed, many cities have neighborhoods dominated by particular racial and ethnic groups. New York's Central Harlem is predominantly African American. East Los Angeles is mainly Latino. South Boston has a lot of Irish Americans. And many cities, like San Francisco, Toronto, Vancouver, and Washington, D.C., have a Chinatown, which is home for immigrants from China, Taiwan, and Vietnam. So as we travel around the city, we come into daily contact with many people who look different from us.

When we perceive racial or ethnic differences, we tend to focus on them. Sometimes we hold negative or even derisive views of certain groups. Other times, we might glamorize or celebrate these differences. In either case, our views are typically based on some stereotype or fantasy of who we expect people to be, based on their presumed race or ethnicity. In such circumstances, we interact with others based on these predetermined judgments rather than actual experience. Even if our judgments are based on past personal experience, they do little to inform us about the individual we're engaging with in the present. Further, our cognitive tendency toward a confirmatory bias means we tend to notice characteristics consistent with our predeterminations and dismiss contradictory evidence. The long-term consequence is that we maintain ethnic and racial stereotypes, contributing to the pernicious realities of racism and discrimination.

Mindfulness provides an opportunity for us to experience people as they truly are, by becoming more aware of our stereotypes. Cultivating an authentic appreciation and understanding of another person promotes mutual respect, and even the development of friendship. Here are a couple of ways to facilitate this process:

- Find someone close by who appears to be from a different racial or ethnic group. Consider things you likely have in common with this person. Perhaps imagine sharing a desire to be happy or win the lottery. Or appreciate your shared experience of the present moment (for example, you're both caught in the rain without an umbrella). Imagine what might make this person laugh. In your mind, extend a blessing, kindness, peace, or good cheer to this person.

- Again, notice someone who seems to have a different race or ethnicity than you do. Bring to mind your assumptions about who this person is, based on apparent group membership. Or recall popular stereotypes of this person's racial or ethnic group. Observe how this person behaves in accordance with—or against—these stereotypes. Consider if and when you've acted the same way in the past, and the degree to which your behavior reflected your ethnicity, personality, circumstances, or some combination of these.

A Line Grows in Brooklyn, or Tokyo, or Los Angeles...

As city dwellers, we spend a lot of time standing in line. We wait to get into the theater, to buy produce at the farmers market, to land a restaurant table, or even to relieve ourselves. Some of the longest—and most distressing—waits are when we're in line to use a portable toilet or the restroom at a bar, restaurant, theater, or stadium.

Typically, we spend our waiting time completely removing ourselves from the present moment. We don't want to wait, so we distract ourselves. Sometimes we completely tune out by reading a book, listening to music, checking e-mail, or playing with our smartphones. Other times, we ruminate on the unpleasantness of waiting by repeatedly checking the status of the line or complaining about others ahead of us in line ("Hey! How can it take you so long to pee?"). We want to rush through this experience to get to more important things.

All of these efforts to distract ourselves or to complain about the length of the wait boil down to dissatisfaction with the present moment. Now is now, whether we like it or not. Jon Kabat-Zinn once remarked that though we're only alive in the present moment, we have the attitude that we only want to be present in the moments we like (Kabat-Zinn and Kabat-Zinn 2009). So what would happen if we tried to bring mindfulness to moments we dislike or experiences we usually try to avoid or rush through, like standing in line? What do you think you would find? The next time you're in line, try some of the following:

- Check in with your body. How's your posture? Do you notice any tension anywhere? What's your facial expression? Are you smiling? Clenching your jaw?

- Examine the thoughts traveling through your mind. Maybe you notice frantic thoughts about what's happening, like "She better move up!" or "Make up your mind and order something already!"

- Resist the temptation to distract yourself. Maybe you notice that your mind doesn't like being still; it wants you to *do* something or, at least, ruminate on something.

- Look at the people around you. Notice the thoughts and judgments that arise. Maybe you start to criticize, praise, or envy those around you. Perhaps you start coveting someone else's place ahead of you in line. Can you find it within yourself to be happy for this person, or do you simply feel resentful?

- Identify something in your immediate experience that sparks some curiosity or satisfaction. Maybe you'll notice an interesting painting on the wall, or realize your headache is gone. Mindfully bring your attention to this experience, by noting what you perceive through your senses or how it feels to embody a particular emotion.

Literally, Why Are You Here?

Cities provide a boundless variety of experiences. We can choose from different cuisines, cultural opportunities, sporting events, museums, and more. We also have the chance to meet many people, visit family or friends, and contribute to diverse communities. Despite all of these options, it's easy to get caught in the same old patterns. We either go to the same places and do the same things, or always stay in. At such times, focusing some awareness on why you live in your particular city at all might help. Presumably, you could live elsewhere, but there must be certain things tying you to this place, like work, family, friends, or the city's environment.

Ask yourself, "Why do I choose to live here?" Already, your judgmental mind might resist this question. "I don't *choose* to live here at all," it argues. "I *have* to live here for my job (or mortgage, partner's career, child's education, or whatever)."

Seeing yourself as a victim of circumstances is certainly no way to feel better. And it's not even accurate, when you get down to it. You clearly have certain priorities, and hopefully, your life reflects most of them. If you live here because you have family nearby, perhaps this value takes precedence over your desire to see the world by boat. If your job keeps you in the city, maybe you place a high priority on your career and finances.

Your reasons for living in the city might be plentiful or boil down to a single one. If you don't even know how to answer this question, consider some of the following possibilities:

- Closeness to (or distance from) family

- Job or career

- Education

- Your child's education

- Cultural options (such as museums, recitals, the opera, movies, and sporting events)

- Diversity of lifestyles and ethnicities

- Friends

- Diversity of foods and cuisines

- Excitement

- Recreational opportunities (such as dancing, clubbing, and so on)

- Athletics (for example, the roller-hockey league and running groups)

Here are some suggestions for further exploring why you've chosen to live in your city:

1. For about thirty minutes, ponder why you live in your city. Consider outlining the pros and cons of living there, or thinking about what keeps you there.

2. Once you've identified your reasons for being where you are, examine the degree to which you've tended to them purposefully. Perhaps you've operated on automatic pilot too long, which has taken you away from your core values. If so, you can start doing more things reflective of what matters most to you. Alternatively, maybe things are going quite well and you've actively pursued what you enjoy and appreciate about your city.

3. In the coming week, pledge to do something in accordance with your reason for living in your city. If you value the wonderful variety of ethnic foods, find a new restaurant to visit. If you enjoy cultural opportunities, visit a museum or see a play.

4. Express gratitude for the opportunity to realize your goals and preferences by living where you do. Maybe there's no one to thank, but you can find ways to thank the city itself by adopting a spirit of good intention or performing an outward act of kindness toward a fellow resident. Even watering one of the municipally owned trees could be a way to say thanks.

Once you've completed these exercises and reconnected with why you're in the city, the challenge lies in maintaining this sense of purpose over time. Feeling dissatisfied or overwhelmed is often a sign that what we're doing in life isn't consistent with our chosen values. So be on the lookout for signs that you have drifted from what you treasure, and explore ways to keep yourself committed to living by the values that are most important to you. Perhaps you can call it "remindfulness": repeatedly assessing the degree to which your current actions reflect your goals and purpose. The alternative—living mindlessly—isn't any easier, and you risk straying far from what's valuable to you. Ideally, you'll cherish each successive moment and find ways to connect to your life experiences. It's trite and true: you have only one life to live. It's up to you to decide what you want to make of it.

References

Allman, L. 1999. The possibilities toolkit: Your guide to better mental health (unpublished group therapy workbook). Augustus F. Hawkins Comprehensive Community Mental Health Center, Los Angeles, CA.

Alicke, M. D., and E. Zell. 2008. Social comparison and envy. In *Envy: Theory and research*, ed. R. H. Smith, 73–93, New York: Oxford University Press.

Baron, N. S. 2008. *Always On: Language in an Online and Mobile World.* New York: Oxford University Press.

Beck, A. T., G. Emery, and R. L. Greenberg. 1985. *Anxiety Disorders and Phobias: A Cognitive Perspective.* New York: Basic Books.

Benson, H., and M. Z. Klipper. 1976. *The Relaxation Response.* New York: HarperTorch.

Berman, M. G., J. Jonides, and S. Kaplan. 2008. The cognitive benefits of interacting with nature. *Psychological Science* 19 (12):1207–12.

Berto, R. 2005. Exposure to restorative environments helps restore attentional capacity. *Journal of Environmental Psychology* 25 (3):249–59.

Boyce, W. T., P. O'Neill-Wagner, C. S. Price, M. Haines, and S. J. Suomi. 1998. Crowding, stress, and violent injuries among behaviorally inhibited rhesus macaques. *Health Psychology* 17 (3):285–89.

Calhoun, J. B. 1962. Population density and social pathology. *Scientific American* 206 (2):139–48.

Campbell-Sills, L., D. H. Barlow, T. A. Brown, and S. G. Hofmann. 2006. Acceptability and suppression of negative emotion in anxiety and mood disorders. *Emotion* 6 (4):587–95.

Chong, H., J. L. Riis, S. M. McGinnis, D. M. Williams, P. J. Holcomb, and K. R. Daffner. 2008. To ignore or explore: Top-down modulation of novelty processing. *Journal of Cognitive Neuroscience* 20 (1):120–34.

References

Crouse, K. 2009. Avoiding the deep end when it comes to jitters. *New York Times*, July 26, sports section.

de Lucia, L. Metropolitan diary. 2008. *New York Times*, November 16, region section. www.nytimes.com/2008/11/17/nyregion/17diary.html?partner=permalink&exprod=permalink (accessed December 4, 2009).

Driskell, J. E., C. Copper, and A. Moran. 1994. Does mental practice improve performance? *Journal of Applied Psychology* 79 (4):481–92.

Dronjak, S., L. Gavrilović, D. Filipović, and M. B. Radojčić. 2004. Immobilization and cold stress affect sympatho-adrenomedullary system and pituitary-adrenocortical axis of rats exposed to long-term isolation and crowding. *Physiology and Behavior* 81 (3):409–15.

Eriksson, P. S., E. Perfilieva, T. Björk-Eriksson, A. M. Alborn, C. Nordborg, D. A. Peterson, and F. H. Gage. 1998. Neurogenesis in the adult human hippocampus. *Nature Medicine* 4 (11):1313–17.

Giaquinto, S., and F. Valentini. 2009. Is there a scientific basis for pet therapy? *Disability and Rehabilitation* 31 (7):595–98.

Griskevicius, V., J. M. Tybur, S. W. Gangestad, E. F. Perea, J. R. Shapiro, and D. T. Kenrick. 2009. Aggress to impress: Hostility as an evolved context-dependent strategy. *Journal of Personality and Social Psychology* 96 (5):980–94.

Hartig, T., G. W. Evans, L. D. Jamner, D. S. Davis, and T. Gärling. 2003. Tracking restoration in natural and urban field settings. *Journal of Environmental Psychology* 23 (2):109–23.

Hill, S. E., and D. M. Buss. 2008. The evolutionary psychology of envy. In *Envy: Theory and research*, ed. R. H. Smith, 60–70. New York: Oxford University Press.

Holmes, E. A., and A. Matthews. 2005. Mental imagery and emotion: A special relationship? *Emotion* 5 (4):489–97.

Kabat-Zinn, J. 1990. *Full Catastrophe Living: Using the Wisdom of Your Body and Mind to Face Stress, Pain, and Illness*. New York: Delta.

————. 1994. *Wherever You Go, There You Are: Mindfulness Meditation in Everyday Life*. New York: Hyperion.

Kabat-Zinn, J., and M. Kabat-Zinn. 2009. Mindful parenting: Cultivating self-awareness, compassion, and understanding. Presentation at Meditation and Psychotherapy: Cultivating Compassion and Wisdom conference, Department of Psychiatry, Cambridge Health Alliance Physicians Organization, at Harvard Medical School Department of Continuing Education, May 2, in Boston, MA.

Kaplan, R., and S. Kaplan. 1989. *The Experience of Nature: A Psychological Perspective*. New York: Cambridge University Press.

Kaplan, S. 1995. The restorative benefits of nature: Toward an integrative framework. *Journal of Environmental Psychology* 15 (3):169–82.

Kaplan, S., L. V. Bardwell, and D. B. Slakter. 1993. The museum as a restorative environment. *Environment and Behavior* 25 (6):725–42.

Kimmelman, M. 2009. At Louvre, many stop to snap, but few stay to focus. *New York Times*, August 2, art and design section.

Kleiber, C., and D. C. Harper. 1999. Effects of distraction on children's pain and distress during medical procedures: A meta-analysis. *Nursing Research* 48 (1):44–49.

Kristeller, J. L., and C. B. Hallett. 1999. An exploratory study of a meditation-based intervention for binge eating disorder. *Journal of Health Psychology* 4 (3):357–63.

Leahy, R. L. 2005. *The Worry Cure: Seven Steps to Stop Worry from Stopping You*. New York: Harmony.

————. 2009. *Anxiety Free: Unravel Your Fears Before They Unravel You*. New York: Hay House.

References

Lohr, V. I., C. H. Pearson-Mims, and G. K. Goodwin. 1996. Interior plants may improve worker productivity and reduce stress in a windowless environment. *Journal of Environmental Horticulture* 14 (2):97–100.

Marlatt, G. A., and J. R. Gordon, ed. 1985. *Relapse Prevention: Maintenance Strategies in the Treatment of Addictive Behaviors.* New York: The Guilford Press.

Mittone, L., and L. Savadori. 2009. The scarcity bias. *Applied Psychology* 58 (3):453–68.

Moore, J. 1999. Population density, social pathology, and behavioral ecology. *Primates* 40 (1):1–22.

National Coffee Association. 2009. National coffee drinking trends 2009. www.ncausa.org/i4a/pages/index.cfm?pageID=647 (accessed October 6, 2009).

Orsillo, S. M., and L. Roemer, ed. 2005. *Acceptance- and Mindfulness-Based Approaches to Anxiety: Conceptualization and Treatment.* New York: Springer.

Park, S-H., and R. H. Mattson. 2008. Effects of flowering and foliage plants in hospital rooms on patients recovering from abdominal surgery. *HortTechnology* 18 (4):563–68.

Post, E. 1922. *Etiquette in Society, in Business, in Politics and at Home.* New York: Funk and Wagnalls.

Ramsden, E. 2009. The urban animal: Population density and social pathology in rodents and humans. *Bulletin of the World Health Organization* 87 (2):82.

Segal, Z. V., J. M. G. Williams, and J. D. Teasdale. 2002. *Mindfulness-Based Cognitive Therapy for Depression: A New Approach to Preventing Relapse.* New York: The Guilford Press.

Serrell, B. 1997. Paying attention: The duration and allocation of visitors' time in museum exhibitions. *Curator* 40 (2):108–25.

Skinner, B. F. 1953. *Science and Human Behavior*. New York: The Macmillan Company.

Slater, A. 2007. Escaping to the gallery: Understanding the motivations of visitors to galleries. *International Journal of Nonprofit and Voluntary Sector Marketing* 12 (2):149–62.

Thich Nhat Hanh. 1991. *Peace Is Every Step: The Path of Mindfulness in Everyday Life*. New York: Bantam Books.

Ulrich, R. S. 1984. View through a window may influence recovery from surgery. *Science* 224 (4647):420–21.

Underhill, P. 1999. *Why We Buy: The Science of Shopping*. New York: Touchstone.

U.S. Environmental Protection Agency, Office of Noise Abatement and Control. 1981. *Noise Effects Handbook: A Desk Reference to Health and Welfare Effects of Noise*. Revised ed. Fort Walton Beach, FL: National Association of Noise Control Officials. www.nonoise.org/library/handbook/handbook.htm (accessed December 11, 2009).

Vormbrock, J. K., and J. M. Grossberg. 1988. Cardiovascular effects of human–pet dog interactions. *Journal of Behavioral Medicine* 11 (5):509–17.

Weingarten, G. 2007. Pearls before breakfast. *Washington Post*, April 8.

Wickelgren, W. A. 1977. Speed-accuracy tradeoff and information processing dynamics. *Acta Psychologica* 41 (1):67–85.

Wu, P-L., and W-B. Chiou. 2009. More options lead to more searching and worse choices in finding partners for romantic relationships on-line: An experimental study. *CyberPsychology and Behavior* 12 (3):315–18.

Yerkes, R. M., and J. D. Dodson. 1908. The relation of strength of stimulus to rapidity of habit formation. *Journal of Comparative Neurology and Psychology* 18 (5):459–82.

Jonathan S. Kaplan, Ph.D., is a clinical psychologist who specializes in the application of mindfulness and meditation to psychotherapy. He founded UrbanMindfulness.org in 2008, and maintains a private practice in New York City where he provides psychotherapy, professional training, and clinical supervision. He lives in Brooklyn with his wife and two children.

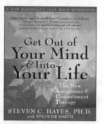